THE REAL READER'S QUARTERLY

Slightly Foxed

'One Man and His Pigs'

NO.62   SUMMER 2019

Editors Gail Pirkis & Hazel Wood
Marketing and publicity Stephanie Allen & Jennie Harrison Bunning
Bookshops Anna Kirk
Subscriptions Hattie Summers

Cover illustration: Chloe Cheese, 'Riverbank Picnic'

Chloe Cheese makes prints, drawings and sometimes illustrations. She was brought up in the Essex village of Great Bardfield but now lives in London where she has been since she graduated from the Royal College of Art in the 1970s. In her work she seeks out the details of daily life and draws them. Follow her on Instagram (@chloeacheese).

Design by Octavius Murray
Layout by Andrew Evans
Colophon and tailpiece by David Eccles

© The contributors 2019

Published by Slightly Foxed Limited
53 Hoxton Square
London N1 6PB

tel 020 7033 0258
email office@foxedquarterly.com
www.foxedquarterly.com

Slightly Foxed is published quarterly in early March, June, September and December

Annual subscription rates (4 issues)
UK and Ireland £48; Overseas £56

Single copies of this issue can be bought for £12.50 (UK) or £14.50 (Overseas)
All back issues in printed form are also available

ISBN 978-1-910898-29-1
ISSN 1742-5794

Printed and bound by Smith Settle, Yeadon, West Yorkshire

Contents

3

Contents

John Watson

The Slightly Foxed Podcast

The first seven episodes of our new podcast are now available. To listen, visit www.foxedquarterly.com/pod or search for Slightly Foxed on Audioboom, iTunes or your podcast app. Future episodes will be available on the 15th of each month.

Subscriber Benefits

Slightly Foxed can obtain any books reviewed in this issue, whether new or second-hand. To enquire about a book, to access the digital edition of *Slightly Foxed* or to view a list of membership benefits, visit www.foxedquarterly.com/members or contact the office: 020 7033 0258 / office@foxedquarterly.com.

From the Editors

Here in the office, summer is when we try to relax a little, draw breath and catch up with the things for which there isn't normally time. This year Jennie and Anna are further improving the website and putting on to the index our entire archive of contributions to past issues, so if you are a subscriber, any piece we've ever published will soon be available for you to read. Meantime we two will be settling down to some quiet reading in our search for unusual and outstanding memoirs to add to the list of Slightly Foxed Editions. We always welcome your suggestions, so if you have a favourite memoir that is now largely unavailable, do get in touch. There are plenty of forgotten memoirs out there we find, but few have that indefinable voice that makes them unique, and it's a real joy when we come across one.

This summer's Slightly Foxed Edition, by our old friend Eric Newby, certainly has that individual voice. *Love and War in the Apennines* (see p. 13) fills in the part of the Newby story that preceded his marriage to Wanda and his brief career in the fashion business which he described so hilariously in *Something Wholesale* (SFE No. 41). Here Newby is an escaped prisoner-of-war in the mountainous Apennines after the Italian government's surrender to the Allies in 1943. Italian peasants risk their lives to shelter him, and it's here that he first meets Wanda, with whom he falls in love, and whose Slovene family help him to escape. The extraordinary story is told in Newby's endearingly jaunty style, but there is no question, as he admits, that the trauma of this experience affected him for the rest of his life. A must for Newby fans, and a treat in store for anyone who hasn't yet encountered him.

We're also looking forward to sharing with readers young and old the first two of Rosemary Sutcliff's great quartet of children's novels set in Roman Britain: *The Eagle of the Ninth*, *The Silver Branch*, *Frontier Wolf* and *The Lantern Bearers*, some of which have long been difficult to find. Many of you will have read them as children: reading them as adults we found ourselves entirely lost again in the haunting atmosphere Sutcliff summons up of the last days of a great empire in this cold British outpost far from Rome. They bring a lost and fascinating world tangibly alive, and we couldn't put them down. We'll be reissuing the first two as *SF* Cubs this autumn, and the other two in September 2020, and we can take advance orders for all of them now.

On 15 June our eighth podcast, in which we'll be discussing the art of travel writing, will be available – like the previous seven – via our website, or any other means you choose. We're delighted that so many of you have written to tell us how much you enjoy the podcasts. After initial nerves at actually being 'on air' we are enjoying them too, opening another window between us and you, and introducing you to more of the life of *Slightly Foxed* and the people who contribute to it. We hope the podcasts will introduce some new readers to *SF* too, so if you are enjoying them, please do put the word about.

A new batch of our popular clothbound *SF* notebooks is also now available. There is a choice of two colours, our attractive signature duck-egg blue and an elegant pale mushroom. They both come, as before, in two sizes: the larger one the size of *Slightly Foxed* itself, and the smaller the size of the Slightly Foxed Editions.

And finally, congratulations to the winner of our writers' competition T. M. Delaney who lives in Orkney. He will receive a prize of £250, and we look forward to publishing his piece soon.

GAIL PIRKIS & HAZEL WOOD

One Man and His Pigs

LAURIE GRAHAM

Many of you will already be acquainted with Clarence Threepwood, 9th Earl of Emsworth. You will know that in a life buffeted by bossy and opinionated women the Earl's greatest consolation is his prize-winning Berkshire sow, the Empress of Blandings. P. G. Wodehouse's Lord Emsworth is a connoisseur of pigs and his favourite book, possibly the only one he ever reads, is *The Care of the Pig* by Augustus Whiffle.

I'm partial to pigs myself. As an asthmatic child of the suburbs I was often packed off to stay with country cousins, in the belief that fresh air would cure me. It didn't. I suspect all that pollen and horse-hair made my asthma worse, but on the positive side I enjoyed a freedom to wander that few children are allowed today, and I became familiar with the sights and smells and facts of country life.

I was mesmerized by the size and stately pace of the cows we brought in at milking time. I learned to be respectful of the capriciousness of horses and I became gruesomely interested in the myriad ways a sheep can find to meet a tragic and premature end. But it was pigs that really drew me.

On one occasion I was invited to visit a maternity sty a couple of weeks after a Large Black had farrowed. She had a litter of eight. 'If you can catch one,' said the pigman, 'you can keep it.' The prospects for a growing pig in my parents' small suburban semi didn't worry him. He knew I'd never hold on to one long enough to claim it. If

James Hogg (ed.), *Lord Emsworth's Annotated Whiffle* (1991), is out of print, but we can obtain second-hand copies.

you've never held a piglet let me tell you, it is a warm and velvety, squirmy bag of squeaks. I was smitten. *Dog person or cat person?* a personality quiz might ask. 'Pig,' I would have to reply.

I grew up, lived in cities, never kept pigs, but they remained my domesticated animal of choice. According to Chinese astrology I was born in a Year of the Pig so, you know . . . You may therefore imagine my excitement when, about twenty years ago, I found, in a bookshop in Charing Cross Road, a copy of *Whiffle's Care of the Pig* edited by James Hogg almost to pocket size and annotated by Lord Emsworth himself.

I never scribble in books. I was brought up to regard book deface-ment as a sin. In our house it was right up there with simony and sorcery. Nevertheless I take vicarious delight in other people's naugh-tiness. Indeed, one of the reasons I married my husband was for his marginalia. It seemed to me that a man who had the gumption to write *Complete bull* and *Fallacy of the undistributed middle!!* in a book by one over-fêted author was a keeper.

So, I had in my hands Whiffle, on pigs, with margin notes by Lord Emsworth. Joy piled upon joy. I coughed up £3.50 and ran home with my treasure. It was a sound investment, destined to become one of my annual go-to books, particularly in the grey days of February when there's nothing much to smile about. A few years ago I men-tioned this fact in a blog post and was astonished to receive a message from the book's editor. Mr Hogg said he had been astonished (a rare case of mutual and almost synchronous astonishment) to learn that anyone even read his book. I know the feeling, as does any writer apart from, say, J. K. Rowling and Robert Ludlum.

But, *revenons à nos cochons*. What exactly is this book? Who, for instance, was its author, Augustus Whiffle? A good question. You might think that a man who composed more than 700 pages on pig husbandry, leaving no pignut unturned, would have been a celebrity, a legend on the after-dinner speech circuit, but no. Mr Whiffle was a creature of the early twentieth century when tweeting was an activity confined to birds. He remains elusive. He was apparently a member of the Athenaeum Club, but that doesn't carry us much further forward. His pig credentials, though, were impeccable. His encyclopaedic knowledge of pigs was learned at the knee of his uncle, Sir Craster Whiffle, and Sir Craster loomed like a colossus over the world of late Victorian piggery. He was a breeder of Lincolnshire Curly Coats (sadly now extinct) and a columnist for the *Lindsey and Kesteven Pig Breeder* for more than sixty years.

There are no Whiffles in my family tree but the village where I was exiled, with orders to stop wheezing and buck up, was on the borders of Leicestershire and Lincolnshire, so I feel a certain geographical affinity.

Another question: which stage of Lord Emsworth's long connection with Whiffle on pigs does this annotated edition reveal? A little detective work suggests that most of the marginalia date from Wellbeloved's second term as head pigman at Blandings. I offer as evidence the following margin notes: *Ask Wellbeloved?* and *Wellbeloved still reluctant to adopt this procedure.* The procedure referred to was Whiffle's recommendation to ascertain a reluctant sow's true feelings vis-à-vis sexual congress by sitting astride her. I'm with Wellbeloved on this point. It sounds like a manoeuvre fraught with risk. Do not try this at home.

Lord Emsworth employed a number of pigmen over the years. George Wellbeloved was undoubtedly his favourite – witness the second chance he was given after an act of unspeakable treachery. Wellbeloved's downfall was strong drink, though in my opinion that in no way mitigated his disloyalty. After Wellbeloved's first departure there was a pigman called Pirbright and another called Potts who had a speech impediment and who, if memory serves, won the football pools and was lured away to the fleshpots of Birmingham.

The most surprising appointment to the Blandings piggery was that of Monica Simmons, a hearty girl who had played hockey for Roedean – Lord Emsworth was in the vanguard of equal-opportunity employ-

Daniel Macklin

ment policy. But Wellbeloved was then given a second bite of the cherry and I believe the *Annotated Whiffle* dates from his second term.

I have learned a lot from this little vade mecum. For instance, that coarse hair on a boar is often indicative of a villainous temper and that skimmed milk tends to make pigs costive. That the assassination of Archduke Franz Ferdinand in 1914 was almost certainly the outcome of a long-festering quarrel between Serbia and Austro-Hungary regarding pork tariffs. And that a bucket of boiled potatoes is guaranteed to mend the broken heart of any young pig when it is time for him to leave his mother. I pass this tip on to any human parents who have a 29-year-old postgraduate weaner still in residence.

Authoritative though he is, I do part company with Whiffle occasionally. For instance, on the topic of piebald pigs. He dismisses them as genetic halfway houses. As a writer who counts a Gloucester Old Spot as one of her most devoted readers, I must demur. An orchard pig can be a master of literary discernment, not to mention a progenitor of peerless porkers with good marbling and a perfect amount of back fat. The Gloucester Old Spot has nothing to apologize for.

Not all pigs are readers, of course. Lord Emsworth's beloved

Empress ate the manuscript of Galahad Threepwood's memoirs when she found it tossed into her sty. How it came to be there is an unsolved mystery. Thrown there by someone envious of its literary merit? Or by someone fearful of exposure by an indiscreet anecdote? The prime suspect was Percy Pilbeam but I remain sceptical. Would a man with shiny, finger-waved hair and a phobia of pigs have ventured anywhere near the Blandings piggery? I think not.

Always interested in examples of pigs in literature – an excellent topic for a thesis if only I had been clever enough to do a Ph.D. – I was very grateful to the *Annotated Whiffle* for the following information. Count Leo Tolstoy, a hugely influential pig breeder in the Tula oblast, south of Moscow, was also something of a weekend scribbler and actually lost several pages of a work in progress, his novella *War and Peace*, when they fell into a grinder and ended up in the swill trough where they were much relished by a herd of Estonian baconers. Count Tolstoy had omitted to keep a back-up copy. There is a lesson there for all would-be writers.

I hesitate to speak of my own literary efforts and only do so to mention the three pigs that adorned the pages of *The Importance of Being Kennedy*. The novel's protagonist, Nora, a Westmeath girl working as a nursery maid to the Kennedy family, reminisces at one point about a pig her parents kept. In Ireland a cottage pig was often referred to as 'yer man who'll help pay the rent'. From Nora's description of the pig's escapades I believe I must have had in mind a Tamworth. They are the very Houdinis of the pig nation.

Later in the same book, with Nora now living in England and experiencing the privations of Second World War rationing, she speaks of her husband, Walter, and his participation in a Pig Club. In a moment of authorial carelessness I failed to identify the breed of a pig named Hermann Goering but my money would be on a Large Black, not dissimilar to Lord Emsworth's Empress but without the distinctive white socks of the Berkshire. Goering was so named by me, as was Nora and Walter's post-war pig, Stalin, in recognition of a need to temper the sadness that inevitably weighs on softer-hearted pig-keepers as the day of doom approaches. Just deserts for Goering and Stalin. Dust to dust, pig to crackling.

I commend Mr Hogg's little book to you on several counts. It contains handy recipes for chitterlings and flead cakes, its modest length belies the wealth of pig lore to be found between its covers, and it includes a useful reference list of characters referred to in Lord Emsworth's annotations, thereby circumventing any need to reread the Blandings novels. But then, why not do that anyway?

LAURIE GRAHAM is not the Canadian Olympic downhill skier, nor is she the Purdue University Director of Women's Studies. She is the other Laurie Graham: novelist, journalist, scriptwriter and pig aficionado. Her novel *The Grand Duchess of Nowhere* was dedicated to Ernest Pig of North Down Farm in Devon.

Daniel Macklin

A Romantic Escape

PATRICK FRENCH

An escaped British prisoner-of-war is sleeping in a grassy hollow by the edge of a cliff. He wakes to find a German soldier standing over him, wearing summer battledress, a pistol at his hip. Realizing he has been caught, he says his name and adds, 'I'm a lieutenant in the infantry, or rather I was until I was put in the bag.' *In the bag* – captured. It is one of the many phrases of the time that add to the resonance of *Love and War in the Apennines* (1971), a vivid memoir of Eric Newby's capture, escape and recapture in Italy's mountainous terrain during the later years of the Second World War. The man standing over him will not, though, take him away. Oberleutnant Frick is an education officer who instead proffers a bottle of beer and talks of his love of butterflies, which he has come to collect in the hills, armed with a net. He says his day job is to give lectures on Italian Renaissance culture 'to groups of officers and any of the men who are interested. It is scarcely arduous because so few of them are.'

This is a book about love, and a book about pain. In evoking his memories of the war, writing twenty-five years after it had ended, Newby was also evoking his knowledge or recollection at the time of the world he had left behind at home, an era of 'volunteer ladies dishing out fish and chips to [soldiers], and great squelchy jam sandwiches, and cups of orange-coloured tea'. A Special Boat Section operative, he was on the run in Italy from the fascist *milizia*. One evening in the depths of winter in 1943, he broke down. The previous few weeks had been passed in a cave, blocked in by snow. Christmas was approaching. He was ill and emaciated, travelling ever higher into the Apennines with a sack of rice and other impromptu supplies:

That night something happened to me on the mountain. The weight of the rice coupled with the awful cough which I had to try and repress broke something in me. It was not physical; it was simply that part of my spirit went out of me, and in the whole of my life since that night it has never been the same again.

The admission brings you up short. *It has never been the same again.* Newby's reserve and good humour, the period English tic that runs through the book of making light of disaster, cover a breaking of the human spirit that altered the rest of his life. The physical and emotional pressure of living in constant danger caught up with him. He was, of necessity, homeless, a beggar, a captive of the frozen mountainous landscape, a vagrant dependent on the goodwill of the local Italian farmers who themselves faced possible execution if they helped a captive on the run. An Allied prisoner-of-war such as Newby could earn his pursuer good money, up to eighteen hundred lire in some parts of Italy.

In this region, people made mattresses out of leaf-covered boughs and cheese from ewe's milk formed into little rounds. They ground chestnuts for flour, dressed in patchwork clothes, whittled new wooden soles to enable shoes to last longer, brewed infusions out of moss to cure an assortment of ailments, and slept beneath sheepskins that still smelt of sheep. Though they had little enough themselves, they were hospitable. One day Newby was given a picnic by a barrel-chested man in a snuff-coloured velveteen suit: nothing, he found, could be more delicious than the '*polenta*, a sort of solidified yellow porridge made from maize, which he sliced with a piece of wire; wonderful hard white bread made from something called *pasta dura* and with it slices of *culatello*, a kind of unsmoked ham from part of the pig's behind that was cut so thinly that it was almost transparent'. The reader is with him now, feeling his excitement at getting fed after months of want.

Newby came from a generation that is today almost extinct, those

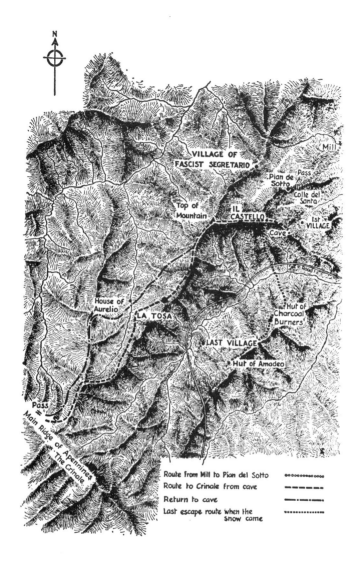

N

VILLAGE OF
FASCIST SEGRETARIO

Mill

Pass

Pian de
Sotto

Colle del
Santa

Top of
Mountain

IL
CASTELLO

1st
VILLAGE

Cave

Road to

House of
Aurelio

Hut of
Charcoal
Burners'

LA TOSA

LAST VILLAGE

Hut of Amadeo

Pass

Main Ridge of Apennines
The Crinale

Route From Mill to Pian del Sotto   ∞∞∞∞∞∞∞∞∞∞

Route to Crinale from cave   ————————

Return to cave   ———.———.—

Last escape route when the   ....
               snow came

who remember the war as it was fought. Born a century ago this year, he had an adventurous life sailing from Australia to Europe on a windjammer as a teenager before joining the Black Watch and later the Special Boat Section. After the war, he was a successful travel writer. In August 1942 while on a secret seaborne mission to bomb a German airfield in Sicily, he was captured and sent to Rome, and then to a building in Fontanellato that had been an *orfanotrofio* or orphanage.

After the Italian government's surrender to the Allies in September 1943, when their Italian captors fled and the Germans were yet to arrive, the British prisoners-of-war in the *orfanotrofio* escaped. They thought their own troops would soon arrive, and Eric Newby dressed specially for the occasion in whipcord trousers, a battledress jacket and a silk muffler. But the moment of liberation was several years away. Newby was hampered by a broken foot, but he was helped by locals whose dislike of fascism made them take terrible risks to protect him. As one man tells him later in the book, some of them have sons fighting in Russia who they know may never return: 'They feel that you are in a similar condition to that of their sons who, they hope, are being given help wherever they are.'

It is this mutual understanding, this symbiosis, that underpins the emotion running alongside the pain in *Love and War in the Apennines*. People step in to help. They hew wood to build a protective cabin. At great risk to themselves children and adults carry food to the visitor, and they have a loyalty to one another that comes from a devotion to freedom, a sense that they are on the same side. Even when Newby becomes a labourer and, in exchange for food and shelter, takes on the Sisyphean task of clearing a farmer's fields of endless stones, tipping them each day from a handcart over a cliff, he writes so wittily it seems almost like a story about a pleasurable rural idyll.

Coming from a pre-war world where feelings were covered by laughter, he articulates jokes that disguise distress. He quotes an officer in the Grenadiers, for example, who refuses to leave his dog behind during an air raid: 'I wouldn't dream of leaving my little girl here. Her nerves are going to pieces.' When Newby and a fellow British escapee hear King George VI on the wireless at Christmas, 'the people in the room witnessed the awful spectacle, something which they are unlikely ever to see again, of two Englishmen with tears running down their cheeks'. Emotion is kept at one remove.

This kind of feeling is accompanied by another sensation that runs through the book: love, not an abstract love of freedom or country, but  romantic love for a woman named Wanda who helped him to escape and who, the reader knows, will become his wife after the fighting ends. She is, along with her parents, an outsider in Italy, a Slovene whose family were deported from territory ceded to Italy after the previous world war. Without the courage of Wanda and her father in exfiltrating Newby by car past a German Panzer division, he would surely have been captured. She sticks by him, remotely. One of the most beautiful moments in the story is when they manage a momentary rendezvous in the mountains, having previously communicated obliquely via coded letters. In another book, *Something Wholesale* (Slightly Foxed Edition No. 41), which preceded *Love and War in the Apennines* and detailed a career diversion into the women's fashion business, Newby describes how he and Wanda were reunited and married in 1946, against all the odds.

Love and War in the Apennines is a moving reminder of a world gone by, and it shows us how a way of life in the more inaccessible regions of Europe has been replaced by forms of modernity that we now take for granted. For many of the people in the mountainous parts of Italy, a neighbour in another valley was an alien, speaking another dialect and practising different customs. The *carbonari*, for instance, the charcoal-burners, their skin blackened by the work, could barely be understood: 'They live their own lives and they speak their own language.' The characters Newby meets on his journey offer a vivid tableau of mid-twentieth-century resilience and invention. One old man, Aurelio, tells him involved tales that he had learned from a storyteller, and there in the remotest part of the northern Apennines he has built a home-made forge out of beaten tin cans and seasoned timber, that enables him to construct a merry-go-round or the axle of a cart. 'When he was young he made a bicycle entirely out of wood, the only part he didn't make was the chain.' People know little of the world outside: for the women at the farm of stones, England is famous only for its monstrous criminals like Dr Crippen and Jack the Ripper, and the legendary London fog.

Love and War in the Apennines is a book of romantic escape, overseen by the suffering of war, which shows how it ripples out across society and into fragile human lives.

PATRICK FRENCH is a historian and biographer whose books have won many prizes. He is presently writing the biography of the Nobel Laureate Doris Lessing.

Eric Newby's *Love and War in the Apennines* (360pp) is now available in a limited and numbered cloth-bound edition of 2,000 copies (subscriber price: UK & Eire £17, Overseas £19; non-subscriber price: UK & Eire £18.50, Overseas £20.50). All prices include post and packing. Copies may be ordered by post (53 Hoxton Square, London N1 6PB), by phone (020 7033 0258) or via our website www.foxedquarterly.com.

Energetic Idleness

ADAM FOULDS

In Nabokov's novel *The Gift* (1938) the young poet Fyodor Godunov-Cherdyntsev is solitary and gifted. A virtuoso of perception, he sees around him many small, delightful details – a shopkeeper's pumpkin-coloured bald spot; an iridescent oil slick on a road with a plume-like twist, asphalt's parakeet – that others around him miss. This capacity makes him one of nature's aristocrats, as Clarence Brown once wrote of the poet Mandelstam, refined, elegant and immeasurably, immaterially rich. He also happens to be a literal aristocrat, a Russian count dispossessed of his estates by the Revolution and living in apparently permanent exile in Berlin in the mid-1930s. He lodges in furnished rooms and scratches a living as a private tutor while his first collection of poems sells a few copies to fellow émigrés.

His girlfriend Zina is perfectly attuned to him emotionally and intellectually and happens to be Jewish. These circumstances might be expected to produce a bitter, strenuous political engagement in Fyodor, but he has only disdain for politics and the wider life of society and keeps his intellect apart, entirely devoted to the 'complex, happy, devout work' of writing that can only be conducted in a state of 'energetic idleness', in 'lofty truancy'. In this, he bears a family resemblance to two other fictional aesthetes of incipient genius, Proust's Marcel and Joyce's Stephen Dedalus.

I was very impressed by Fyodor as a teenager and longed to join that prickly cohort of arch individualists, to write poems of lasting

Vladimir Nabokov, *The Gift* (1938) · Trans. Michael Scammell
Penguin · Pb · 416pp · £10.99 · ISBN 9780141185873

value myself, and to live in that repetition of aesthetic bliss to which they were all committed. I read a great deal of Nabokov. He was one of the few prose writers whose work had the concentrated richness of poetry, my preferred form, and I was bewitched by his brilliance, his dashing, unashamed intelligence and the comprehensive dislike he has for received opinion and group activity that makes liking him feel like a rising above. Recently, though, I've found him harder to read, his formal games impressive but uninteresting. This is a matter of taste only: I am bored by anagrams and metatextual jokes, and would take a single Isaac Babel short story over the heftiest Pynchon novel.

After his switch from Russian to English, Nabokov wrote in a language in which he was divorced from the demotic and his pavonine prose lacks the animating speech rhythms, the sense of breath and natural cadence, that are always present in Joyce, Lawrence, Bellow and Woolf. Rather than being earthed beside us, his prose genius seems airborne above us, swooping and gliding.

So it is interesting to return to *The Gift* now and find that this novel still mesmerizes me for long stretches and to wonder whether a Fyodor Godunov-Cherdyntsev could come into being at all in our present moment with its materialism and saturating pop culture, its social media and monetized interruptions. Fyodor's disdain for general thought and its clichés is absolute and extends even to literature that makes any schematic inferences about society or displays any overt political affiliation. Nabokov's own hatred of the political is well known, but I think it is possible to perceive in his abstention an implied politics: an aristocratic liberalism that is in favour of the humane and the particular and that affirms Isaiah Berlin's negative liberty, the freedom from coercion and oppression. *The Gift*, uniquely, I think, in Nabokov's work, reveals how erudite and thought through his position really was, even as it typically refuses to be explicit.

The Gift is altogether an erudite book. Its heroine is not Zina, Nabokov tells us in his 1962 preface to the first English translation, but Russian literature. It was the last novel he wrote in Russian before his switch to English and it is saturated with references to Russian writers he admires – Pushkin, Gogol, Lermontov, Nekrasov, Chekhov, Tolstoy, Turgenev, Fet, Blok, Bunin and others – as well as a group of primarily political, materialist writers of the 1860s – Chernyshevsky, Dobrolyubov and Pisarev – whom he deplores. You don't have to be well-read in Russian literature to enjoy *The Gift* but it certainly helps, to catch, for example, the imagistic accuracy of this line: 'Dostoevsky always brings to mind somehow a room in which a lamp burns during the day.'

Comprising five long chapters of varying, overlapping focus, *The Gift* is circular rather than linear in design, allowing the reader to dwell in Fyodor's life and mind for a while rather than follow him on a particular adventure. The novel ends with Fyodor conceiving in a lucid, exhilarated rush of ideas the novel that we have just read and promising to write it in the future.

During the course of *The Gift*, we're given several opportunities to read Fyodor's writing, both poetry and prose. In chapter one, hearing of a good review, Fyodor rereads his collection of poems, all neatly turned scenes of childhood, and reminisces around them, his memories thereby presented in both fluid and crystalline form. In his later memoir, *Speak, Memory*, Nabokov talks of his 'hypertrophied sense of lost childhood'. The same passionate nostalgia pervades Fyodor's poems. They are the form taken by his grief for a lost home, family unity and a way of life. As a result, they are perhaps too sweet. Evelyn Waugh, who wrote *Brideshead Revisited* during the privations of the Second World War, said afterwards that, 'with a full stomach', he found its ornamental language distasteful.

In fact, there is a strain of earnest lyricism that runs through all of *The Gift* and that may be too much for some. Beauty seems to exist as a separate, usually visual and highly coloured, category of experience, distilled in such phrases as 'the sunset cloudlets were trimmed with flamingo down'. Too much of this stuff and the reader can feel as if they've eaten too much cake. The same high sugar content can be found in the romance between Fyodor and Zina with its faultless, high-minded mutual understanding and surging throb of lyrical feeling. 'She fell silent, and Fyodor cautiously kissed her burning, melting, sorrowing lips.' His sincere evocation of romantic perfection, to my mind, fails to convince, though later this failure will be transmuted into the success of *Lolita* in which Humbert Humbert's great arias of evocation and passion for Dolores Haze ring both true and false in exactly the right way.

The news of the celebratory review of Fyodor's poems turns out to have been an April Fool's joke. *The Gift* is superb in dealing with the indignities as well as the exaltations of a young writer's life. It matches Joyce in its depiction of a mind besotted with language, listening in to words and their possibilities, often in precise and technical terms.

With equal precision, the psychology of young, insurgent literary ambition is anatomized. Fyodor at one point agonizes over the success of a contemporary,

> a man whose every new searing line he, Fyodor, despising himself, quickly and avidly devoured in a corner, trying by the very act of reading to destroy the marvel of it – after which for two days or so he could not rid himself either of what he had read or of his own feeling of debility or of a secret ache, as if while wrestling with another he had injured his own innermost, sacrosanct particle.

There are excellent portraits of second-rate poets and writers, too, gathered at an émigré literary evening, intoning *symboliste* or neo-classical nonsense with great solemnity.

Chapter four consists entirely of Fyodor's work, his wayward and brilliant biography of Chernyshevsky, a hero of the Bolsheviks, exiled in the nineteenth century, and the author of the earnestly incompetent novel *What Is to Be Done?* In *The Gift*, he is also an ancestor of the couple whose literary evening we attended in chapter one. Fyodor, like Nabokov, disavows politics for its abstraction, its distance from the reality of original sensory experience. This is succinctly put in the description of a character earlier in the novel.

> Like many unpaid windbags he thought that he could combine reports he read in the papers by paid windbags into an orderly scheme, upon following which a logical and sober mind . . . could with no effort explain and foresee a multitude of world events . . . France was AFRAID of something or other and therefore would never ALLOW it. England was AIMING at something. This statesman CRAVED a rapprochement . . .

In his biography, Fyodor mocks Chernyshevsky the socialist materialist for his disconnection from the material world, his clumsiness and myopia, his inability to tell plants apart. Communists throughout the novel are mocked for their physical infirmities, their ugly incapacity or bourgeois stupidity. The participants in a rally are described as 'battered by life, some crookbacked, others lame or sickly, a lot of plain-looking women and several sedate petty-bourgeois'. As well as being reprehensible for its equation of disability or unattractiveness with moral debasement, this is simply crude thought, unworthy of Nabokov. In the Chernyshevsky chapter, we come across passages that by contrast display a great deal of knowledge about political and philosophical thought:

> the political regime that was supposed to appear as the synthesis in the syllogism, where the thesis was the commune, resembled not so much Soviet Russia as the utopias of the day. The world of Fourier, the harmony of the twelve passions, the bliss of collective living, the rose-garlanded workmen – all this could not fail to please Chernyshevsky, who was always looking for 'coherency'. Let us dream of the phalanstery living in a palace: 1,800 souls and all happy!

Much as he liked to dissemble the fact, it seems that Nabokov knew very well whereof he chose not to speak. The Chernyshevsky chapter was not included in the original publication of the novel in the late 1930s, rejected as a character assassination of an important figure, the same reason it is rejected by an editor within the novel, 'a pretty example of life finding itself obliged to imitate the very art it condemns', as Nabokov put it in his later preface.

Here Nabokov is taking pleasure in the patterning of otherwise humanly regrettable material. *The Gift* is a rich lesson in the redeeming value of such pleasure and its abundance, if you know how to pay attention. Fyodor may have lost his home and – like Nabokov, though in different circumstances – his father, and be without any obvious cause for hope, but he loves the world unstintingly. In the final chapter, he notices many beautiful things as he walks through Berlin in good weather, sparkles of sunlight on the street, a disintegrating cloud of train steam, the 'wonderful poetry of railroad banks'.

Where shall I put all these gifts with which the summer morning rewards me – and only me? Store them up for future books? Use them immediately for a practical handbook: How to Be Happy? Or get behind all this, behind the play, the sparkle, the thick, green greasepaint of the foliage? For there really is something, there is something! And one wants to offer thanks but there is no one to thank.

Despite all their losses, Nabokov and Fyodor know how to be happy. Their gifts of perception and patterning reveal the world to them and console furthermore with intimations of something mysterious beyond delightful appearances, something that is gentle and wonderful and benign. Whether we are persuaded by this metaphysical implication or not, *The Gift* convinces that keeping faith with direct personal experience and the making of art, beautiful, tender, useless art, is of inestimable value.

ADAM FOULDS is a poet and novelist. In 2013, he was named as one of Granta's Best of Young British Novelists. His new novel, *Dream Sequence*, has just been published.

Hoofing It

RICHARD CONYNGHAM

Five years ago, on the side of a dirt road in the high Andes, I bought a donkey. Watching me hand a wad of crumpled *soles* to the farmer, my Ecuadorian friend Ramiro smiled and shook his head. 'Are you sure you want to do this, *amigo*, when there are plenty of trucks and buses?' It was a good question, especially considering the pitiful, mud-caked specimen that stood before us. The trouble was, my solo bicycle trip through Latin America had been interrupted by an inflamed knee, but I was determined to continue south without using motorized transport.

Unable to pedal but still able to walk, I had found inspiration in a battered copy of *Eight Feet in the Andes* wedged between the clothes and the spare tubes in my pannier. In the early 1980s, its author Dervla Murphy flew to Cajamarca in Peru with her 9-year-old daughter Rachel. Already a veteran of odysseys on foot, mule, donkey and bicycle, the Irish travel writer needed no justification for what came next. Putting the local grapevine to good use, she and Rachel purchased a lively young mule named Juana. Then, using William Prescott's *History of the Conquest of Peru* as their guidebook, they embarked on a southward trek, following the route of Pizarro's conquistadors all the way to the historic Inca capital of Cuzco.

Incredibly, Rachel was already something of a hardened traveller. Before primary school, she had tagged along in *On a Shoestring to Coorg* (1976), her mother's memoir of a trip to south India. In *Where*

Dervla Murphy, *Eight Feet in the Andes* (1983)
John Murray · Pb · 320pp · £9.99 · ISBN 9780719565168

Dervla and Rachel, taken five years after their Andean journey

the Indus Is Young (1977), she then rode Hallam, an ex-polo pony, for a wintry month in Baltistan. Now, the challenge ahead for the Murphys and their latest steed was on another level: between Cajamarca and Cuzco, their 'eight feet' would need to traverse 1,300 miles of rugged Andean *cordillera*.

Juana was 'an elegant, glossy young lady with an intelligent expression: about 12.1 h. h. and a dark bay, shading off on belly and legs to a most unusual creamy-russet'. My new purchase was comically shorter. Her coat was coffee-brown, overgrown and matted, and with her dreary demeanour she looked sad even by donkey standards. Still, my hope was that by lugging my tent, sleeping bag and two small sacks of clothes across the greater part of Ecuador, this unlikely companion could at least play an important recuperative role in my journey to Tierra del Fuego. And for this reason I named her Remedios, 'Remedies', or Remy for short.

On a crisp morning we set off in ceremonial fashion from the national Equator monument, north-east of Quito. Two days later, we arrived at La Compania, a dilapidated family hacienda that Ramiro was restoring. Having covered barely 20 miles in 20 exhausting hours, I collapsed on a couch, ready to give up. I had expected bouts of sulkiness and obstinacy, but my donkey's aversion to puddles, narrow paths, ankle-deep streams and yellow painted lines filled me with despair. What had I got myself into?

Short on answers, I returned to *Eight Feet* and was soon marvelling once more at Dervla's ability to endure day after long hard day on foot, navigating ravines, vanishing paths and erratic weather. Somehow, even in the bitter cold or pitched awkwardly on a vertiginous incline, she still retained what her publisher Jock Murray described as 'that over-riding determination to put words on paper and the stamina to do it'.

The titles of her diary entries alone – 'camp on ledge of steep mountain' or 'camp on floor of village post office' – were enough to inspire renewed enthusiasm. More than any other travel writer I had encountered, here was the genuine article. Dervla's 'mania for going off into the wilderness' – to use Rachel's words – was her way of reaching out to the past, 'far out over that chasm created in human history by the earthquake of Progress', to the few remaining places on earth untarnished by modernity.

An only child, born in County Waterford in 1931, Dervla was from a young age intoxicated by the world beyond her reach. Poring over her cherished second-hand atlas, a gift from her grandfather, she longed to see not only faraway places with unpronounceable names but also the unmarked spaces between them. In her teens, however, she was pulled out of school to nurse her severely arthritic mother, and only sixteen years later, on the death of both parents, could she finally begin to make up for lost time. Her first book, *Full Tilt* (1965), is an exuberant account of her solo bicycle ride from Ireland to India. She has since written another two dozen, most of them memoirs of journeys through some of the world's most inaccessible regions.

With my spirits restored, Remy and I struck out once more. Ahead lay a 400-mile trek through Ecuador's 'avenue of the volcanoes' to the

Inca ruin of Ingapirca. To escape the Pan-American highway and its tarmac tributaries, we took our first leaf out of *Eight Feet*, tacking deeper into the mountains where footpaths and zigzagging jeep tracks connect the country's most far-flung hamlets. On the way, the experiences of Dervla and Rachel three decades earlier informed my appreciation of the high sierra, its people and their harrowing history.

Often with scarcely enough provisions to sustain themselves, and endlessly on the lookout for Juana's fodder of choice, alfalfa (or 'Alf' in Murphy-speak), the trio adopted an old Dervla approach: in remote areas, depend on the locals. Since the nights she had spent with peasant families in *Full Tilt*, she had learnt that cultural barriers tend to give way to human kindness – and the people of the Peruvian highlands were no exception, even if they came across as aloof, or dulled by a lifetime of coca-chewing.

Both mother and daughter kept diaries, and with good reason Dervla draws repeatedly on Rachel's version of events:

> Mummy wanted to go up the mountain on a little mines track because she pretened [*sic*] that she thought it was a short cut but I had the strong feeling it was just because she wanted to climb to the top. I refused firmly, and I am sure if Juana could have talked she would have thoroughly agreed with me.

Rachel's pragmatism and pluck combined with Dervla's curiosity and endearing self-deprecation ('As we ate, the standard debate about my gender took place among staff and customers') all make for delightful, unpredictable reading. In observing the symptoms of a wider tragedy set in motion by the Spanish conquest 450 years earlier, Dervla is also candid about the demoralized psyche of the Peruvian peasant. And yet, as readers familiar with the Murphy *oeuvre* will know, what stands out more than anything is her tireless fascination with the world, whether she is contemplating the demise of a once-great Incan empire or counting the shades of mountain blue in the distance.

As Remy and I progressed, Juana and the Murphys were always with us in spirit. Together we meandered south, up and down mountainsides, pausing now and then to admire a smoking volcano or a shock of bright pink quinoa, or to ask a *campesino* in a colourful shawl and felt fedora whether we were still on the right track. For them, like me, the highs were literal. After each lung-busting ascent came the euphoria of summiting, when the Andes spread out majestically beneath. 'In three directions we were overlooking hundreds of miles of convulsed Andean splendour – a sort of madness of mountains, possessing the earth to the farthest horizons. "Everywhere is *below* us!" exclaimed Rachel.'

Like Juana, Remy's performance improved with each week. Her pace picked up, and sometimes we covered 20 miles in a day. Right to the end, however, we also shared the sort of desperate, undignified low points that one tends to keep within the family. After a particularly precarious descent, Dervla recalled Juana putting on 'a classic and totally understandable display of mulishness':

> She stood legs braced, ears flattened and eyes rolling expressively towards the depths of the ravine where a torrent foamed noisily between cottage-sized boulders. I had to lead her down, applying a judicious mixture of wheedling and abuse, depending on how appalling our immediate situation was when she chose to be bolshie. 'Actually she's *not* being bolshie,' said Rachel, who was slithering along behind. 'She's just being sensible. This *isn't* a mule track.'

Remy and I reached rock-bottom when we were compelled to use a derelict train tunnel to avoid an unclimbable hill. For as long as the rusted tracks were still visible, I tried to preserve a measure of normality, scratching her ears and humming along merrily. The illusion was soon broken, however, when the tunnel curved away from the dying light. Sensing danger, Remy suddenly dug in her hooves. I tried reason, insisting that I too was scared. When that failed, I had no choice but to push her. In pitch darkness, we inched forward in exhausting bursts, Remy's front hooves churning through the gravel like twin ploughs. Finally we reached a point where she must have realized that the way ahead was no more terrifying than the way back, and she broke away in a hopeful canter while I lay panting in the gloom.

When we finally did reach Ingapirca after more than a month together above 8,000 feet, it was hard not to feel a great affection for my disobliging companion. Happily, my knee was now back in full working order. Remy had been my remedy after all – now it was my turn to be hers. When Dervla and Rachel arrived in Cuzco after a near-catastrophic final stretch, they too were determined to secure a toil-free retirement for their beloved Juana. For them, emancipation lay in a visit to the local tourist office; for me, in Ramiro's willingness to contact every animal lover in his address book.

The last time I saw Remy she was standing in a field, surrounded by excited children, on a family farm near the city of Cuenca. Stripping a bail of Alf with her latest acquaintance, a llama named Chocolaté, she felt no inclination to look up when I announced my departure. Perhaps she had learnt from Dervla's closing words: '*Not saying goodbye is always much easier.*'

After his Ecuadorian ramble, RICHARD CONYNGHAM progressed southwards to the tip of Patagonia by bicycle, along the way tracing the Murphys' route to Cuzco as closely as he could.

Extremely Likeable People

URSULA BUCHAN

In the kind of house where books are handed down the generations, the chances are that on a spare bedroom bookshelf, squeezed between *Guy Mannering* and *Roses, Their Culture and Management*, you will find a copy of one of the eleven novels written by O. Douglas. Take it to bed to read and you will quickly become immersed in the cultured, if circumscribed, Scottish middle-class life of three generations ago. Whether that appeals to you will probably depend both on your attitude to Scotland and Scottishness and on whether you enjoy a well-told if old-fashioned story where only rarely does anything very startling happen.

O. Douglas was the pseudonym of Anna Buchan (1877–1948), one of six children of the Reverend John Buchan and his wife Helen and the only daughter to live to womanhood. She was the sister of John Buchan, author of a hundred books of fiction and non-fiction, including *The Thirty-Nine Steps*. She lived most of her adult years with her mother and bachelor brother, Walter – lawyer, bank agent, town clerk and procurator fiscal – in a house in Peebles, the Border town that she called Priorsford in her novels. Her father, born in Peebles, was a saintly Free Kirk minister, who spent many years working in the slums of the Gorbals in Glasgow and died of overwork soon after retirement. Her mother was of local sheep-farming stock, so the children grew up to be at ease in the diverse environments of rural upper Tweeddale (God's own country, if ever there was one),

---

O. Douglas's novels are out of print but we can obtain second-hand copies.

the self-sufficient, self-respecting town of Peebles and the bustling Victorian city of Glasgow.

Anna was a classic daughter of the manse, involved in every kind of church work, but she was also a talented amateur actress, well-known locally for her comedic turns and poetry recitations. It was not until after her father died in 1911, however, that she began seriously to write, her first published effort being a fictionalized account of the six months she had spent in India with another brother, Willie, who was in the Indian Civil Service.

Olivia in India, told in the first person, is the story of an unmarried Scotswoman of genteel upbringing called Olivia Douglas, who spends six months visiting her ICS brother in Calcutta. Having read Willie Buchan's letters home, it is plain to me that Anna essentially recounted experiences that she herself had enjoyed, especially travelling 'up-country' with her brother, since she was notably doughty and game for anything. *Olivia in India* was published under the name 'O. Douglas' (since Anna refused to ride on her brother John's coat-tails) by the ultra-respectable firm of Hodder & Stoughton in 1913, it having first received the blue-pencil treatment from John, who at the time was a partner in the Scottish publishing company of Thomas Nelson & Sons.

The review in the *Glasgow Herald* noted: 'The author has the great gift of original observations, together with a quiet reflective turn of mind . . . She sees everything with a fresh outlook. She has good humour and a quick gift for catching and describing in expressive form the salient characteristics of persons and places. To have read this book is to have learned much of Anglo-Indian life and to have met an extremely likeable person in the author.'

Even when they first appeared, O. Douglas's novels – of which the most readable are probably *The Setons*, *Penny Plain*, *Pink Sugar*, *Eliza for Common* and *Priorsford* – were advertised as 'nice'. They are certainly innocent, uncynical and very far from knowing. But they are saved from the charge of being saccharine by her sense of humour, which could be acerbic, as well as by a percipience about human nature and a broad, but unsentimental, sympathy.

The female characters are usually principled, often well-meaning, sometimes dowdy, always class-conscious, Scottish provincial women, who delight in a luncheon party in a neighbour's house, are addicted to performing small acts of kindness, are thoroughly at home with the Old Testament and think a good deal about their 'latter end'. The heroines, rather fewer in number, are comfortably off but never patronizing or snobbish and they employ sharp-tongued but kindly servants, who pronounce over small happenings like a Lallans-speaking Greek chorus. (Anna had a very good ear for the cadences and picturesqueness of Scots dialect.) The most unsympathetically portrayed characters are vulgar social climbers or malicious gossips. Most of the books were written after the Great War, so the women often have sorrows to hide, and do not always rejoice with neighbours in their good fortune.

Anna Buchan with her brother John, 1932
(courtesy of the John Buchan Story Museum)

Several of the stories are romances, in the sense that the heroine accepts a proposal of marriage in the final pages, but the male characters rarely make much convincing impact on the story. Any children are encouraged by understanding, patient grown-ups, say funny things, love dogs and act Shakespeare scenes at the drop of a hat. For O. Douglas, the best kind of house is old, with white-painted panelled walls, highly polished old furniture, vases of garden flowers, bright fires and masses of books. Here modest, self-denying, charitable, hard-working people quote poetry and the Bible, sing Border ballads and enjoy afternoon tea more than any other meal. She was describing pretty accurately her own house and family.

It would be misleading, however, to say that O. Douglas's fiction was simply and wholly an extended memoir with just the names changed, although the preface to her autobiography, *Unforgettable, Unforgotten*, might lead one to suppose that she at least thought so: 'My brother John used to say that when he wrote stories he invented, but that I in my books was always remembering.' She was a proper novelist, but she drew so heavily on her family's experiences that it is, for example, obvious that she is thinking of John in *Eliza for Common*, when 'Jimmie', the older brother, comes back to the manse in Glasgow from Oxford after his first term, with several published articles already under his belt and with an Oxford accent, which makes his hurly-burly younger brothers laugh.

The only daughter of the house is plainly Anna herself as a discontented teenager, bullied by her dynamic mother to take an active part in church life, including visiting the poor, but happiest when curled up in a chair reading *As You Like It*. *The Setons* contains an accurate and affectionate portrait of her father, while *Ann and Her Mother* is a gossamer-thin fictionalization of her mother's life. O. Douglas was keen to recreate the particular magic of her upbringing but may also have been wary of straying too far from her own experience, lest she fall into error.

The 1920s and '30s, when her books sold best, were not safe and cosy times and, although she rarely wrote of current affairs – except, for example, to say something approving of Mr Baldwin, a friend of her brother's – she did deal with contemporary preoccupations: the plight of unemployed miners in Fife; aristocratic families losing male heirs in the war and having to sell up; teenagers dying of consumption; slum dwelling in Glasgow. Anna knew a great deal about sorrow: her sister died in early childhood, her brother Willie succumbed to an infection picked up in India before the Great War and her youngest brother, Alastair, was killed at the Battle of Arras. Nevertheless, there is a sober optimism about her books, and many readers, beset by worries about unemployment or incurable sickness, will have been consoled when they immersed themselves in stories about decent, good-hearted people who, to paraphrase John Betjeman, never cheated, never doubted and wrote voluminous monthly letters to their friends and relations.

The novel you are most likely to come across, if only because it has been reissued in recent years, is *Pink Sugar*, which was dedicated to John and his wife Susie, 'because of Bill'. The main child character, 'Bad Bill', a little boy of angelic looks and devilish naughtiness, was based on her nephew, William, my father. A real-life example of this naughtiness, the biting of a housemaid's leg while he was pretending to be a crocodile, makes its way into the book. Anna promised her nephew a farthing for every copy of the first edition that was sold, and the boy made £25; even successful modern novelists would be more than content with a first print run of 24,000 copies.

Anna depended heavily on John Buchan for encouragement and advice, even after she became a well-established author with a large and international fan base. He read her manuscripts, crossing out the indiscriminate 'quotes' to which she was addicted and commenting that some passages were 'incorrigibly noble'. It is a family joke that she must have forgotten that the title of her autobiography – *Unforgettable, Unforgotten* – was prefaced by 'thrilling-sweet and rotten' and referred to the river smell of the Cam in Rupert Brooke's poem 'The Old Vicarage, Grantchester'.

Modernism in fiction writing passed her by completely but, as *The Scotsman* commented at her death, the 'pleasantness' of her writing was a relief to many. In *Pink Sugar*, the lady novelist character remarks: 'The world is full of simple plain people who like plain things, and who are often very bewildered and unhappy. Perhaps my books are a sort of soothing syrup, I don't know.'

Certainly Hodder & Stoughton were most enthusiastic about the syrup. Indeed, O. Douglas and John Buchan became a notable publishing double-act in the 1920s, Hodder's bringing out their books, in a blaze of newspaper publicity, at the same time each summer, just before the book-buying public began their holidays. In 1924, the books were *Pink Sugar* and *The Three Hostages*, in 1926 *The Proper Place* and *The Dancing Floor*.

O. Douglas's novels were particularly popular with expatriate Scots, a race famous for travelling to the undiscovered ends while remaining unassuageably homesick. During the Second World War, my father encountered a rugged, hard-drinking, Scottish tea planter in India who was thrilled to meet a nephew of O. Douglas, since his chief recreation was reading and rereading her books and writing her fan letters. In 1935, when John Buchan was appointed Governor-General of Canada, he was teasingly informed that, among Canadians of Scottish descent, he would be known as O. Douglas's brother.

Having written her last novel, *The House that Is Our Own*, in 1940, Anna spent the rest of the war travelling widely to give lectures and recitations in aid of war charities. By the time she died in 1948, her star was probably already fading. Virginia Woolf's father Leslie Stephen wrote that a 'classic' novel was one that was still read a hundred years after it was written. None of Anna's novels is 'classic' by that standard but they mostly repay reading, if only because they reveal the authentic virtues of a provincial life, where there is a lively sense of the significance of the everyday, a good-natured acceptance of the duty to be kind and generous, and the apprehension of the imminence of judgement – whether by neighbours or by God.

URSULA BUCHAN regrets never having met O. Douglas, or indeed her brother John, whose biography she has recently completed for Bloomsbury.

Antipodean Alcatraz

CHARLES ELLIOTT

Australia was born as a jail. Not until well into the eighteenth century was Europe aware of the place, and even then nobody could see
much use for it. But the British, who claimed it, had serious prob-
lems at home, principal among them being an apparent crime wave
that had generated an unmanageable volume of convicts. What with
poverty, gin and social disorder, justice had become rough indeed –
stealing a loaf of bread might get you hanged. Good citizens were
convinced that a true 'criminal class' was about to engulf the country.
'The huge, ramifying tree of English criminal law', as Robert Hughes
describes it, had left the Georgian government at a loss for ways to
punish so many threatening malefactors.

What to do about it? In *The Fatal Shore* (1986), Hughes's account
of the founding of Australia, we learn about the chosen solution:
transportation. With too many convicts to hang, and no peniten-
tiaries to put them in, the answer was to ship them about as far away
from England as could be devised. What better place than Australia,
presumably secure and empty of people? Thus in 1787 the First Fleet
('this Noah's Ark of small-time criminality') set off for Botany Bay
(ending up in Sydney Cove); before the practice of transportation
was abolished, 162,000 men, women and children would be similarly
dispatched to this Antipodean Alcatraz. Where they came from, why
they were sentenced, what happened to them in this strange new

Robert Hughes, *The Fatal Shore: A History of the Transportation of Convicts to
Australia, 1787–1868* (1986)
Vintage · Pb · 720pp · £12.99 · ISBN 9780099448549

(and often brutal) world, and how, out of pain and chaos, a nation slowly came into existence – it's an enormous story that justifies the scale (700-plus pages) of the book telling it. You don't need to care about Australia to find it gripping.

It is impossible to do justice to *The Fatal Shore* by simply giving its outlines. Hughes covers the Georgian social scene, the workings of English law, the voyage out (which lasted months), the administrators and their methods, the travails of escapees and the develop-ment of an Australian class structure. He describes the con-tested and long-delayed end to the system, signalled by the landing of the last ship in 1868. These large historical themes come to life through the mar-shalling of countless anecdotes, quotations from convicts' let-ters and documents, and des-criptive accounts of everything from the Cumberland Hunt in

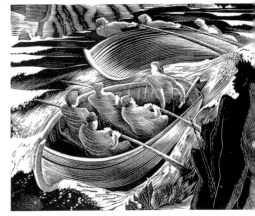

Peter Barker-Mill, wood engraving, from *The First Fleet* (Golden Cockerel Press, 1937)

1820s Sydney going 'baying, belling and tallyhoing after dingoes' to exactly what it was like to receive 100 lashes.

Not every poor convict was exiled for no more than the theft of a couple of handkerchiefs, but some were, and Hughes writes of them with often savage sympathy. Thomas Chadwick, for example, trans-ported for destroying twelve cucumber plants, 'went to Australia, there to contemplate the exactness with which the god of property had measured out his bleak life in cucumbers'. Others were political victims (usually Irish, some Scottish), while some were frankly vil-lains fully deserving of the appalling challenges they faced on landing. At first it was starvation – nobody had bothered to survey the land before sending the convicts – and the most basic absence of shelter.

Then and afterwards there was the overriding problem of discipline, solved in the simplest and cruellest way by use of the lash. During the whole era of transportation, the administration was mainly in the hands of men no better than the worst of their charges. The New South Wales Corps (better known as the Rum Corps) not only took control of the whole colony and monopolized smuggling but also managed to forcibly depose a governor before it was disbanded.

If the first penal settlement in Sydney was not bad enough, the authorities soon found ways of creating worse ones. Norfolk Island, a speck of land a thousand miles to the east of the mainland, became a prison for incorrigibles and notable for the degree of sadism practised there. Moreton Bay, Port Macquarie, Newcastle, all 'hamlets of punishment', sprang up along the coast to the north. What would be the true nexus for the penal system, however, was far to the south on the island then called Van Diemen's Land. A testament to its reputation as a place of misery is the fact that when transportation finally ended, its inhabitants insisted on changing its name to the one it now bears, Tasmania. 'This small hole in the world about the size of Ireland', in Hughes's words, swallowed more than seven out of every ten people shipped from Britain as convicts.

I was in Tasmania a couple of years ago as a tourist, and found it hard to imagine this essentially bucolic, rain-swept country as the place of real suffering Hughes makes plain it was. William Sorell, who took over its administration in 1816, declared in a memo to Sydney that it held 'a larger portion, than perhaps ever fell to the same number in any Country, of the most depraved and unprincipled people in the Universe'. To deal with them the authorities set up such grim establishments as Macquarie Harbour on the west coast of the island and Port Arthur, an isolated prison perched above cliffs at the far extremity of the Tasman Peninsula. Hughes brilliantly describes the approach to this terrifying place:

From Cape Direction, where Australia's oldest lighthouse still winks its beam, the long humpy profile of the Tasman Peninsula lies on the south-eastern horizon. Its furthest southern point is Cape Raoul, which as one rounds it appears as the western arm of Maingon Bay, the sea-gate that opens the way to Port Arthur – the eastern arm being Cape Pillar. Both capes are of towering basalt pipes, flutes and rods, bound like fasces into the living rock. Seabirds wheel, thinly crying, across the black walls and the blacker shadows. The breaking swells throw up their veils. When the clouds march in from the Tasman Sea and the rainsqualls lash the prismatic stone, these cliffs can look like the adamantine gates of Hell itself. Geology had conspired with Lieutenant-Governor Arthur to give the prisoners of the crown a moral fright as their ships hauled in.

Few prisoners ever got back to England after serving their sentences. Most who survived stayed on as 'emancipists', as farmers, stockmen or tradesmen. Many tried, generally unsuccessfully, to escape confinement, although enough did so to create a whole body of legends about bushrangers and other backwoods marauders. Some, possessing a dangerously inadequate grasp of geography, headed north on foot intending to walk to China; one carried a compass drawn on a piece of paper. But there were a few truly intrepid characters who did manage to flee.

Mary Bryant was transported for seven years for stealing a cloak. In 1791, along with her two children, her fisherman husband and seven other convicts, she sneaked out of Sydney under cover of night in a small open boat. Contending with storms, shipwreck, starvation and skirmishes with natives, the party made it all the way to Timor, where they were thrown into detention and shipped off to the Dutch East Indies in irons. Bryant's husband and one child died there, of fever. The diminished party, now in English hands, was sent back to the Cape and finally on to England; en route Mary's daughter succumbed. At this point Mary's prospects seemed limited to prison and a second voyage back to captivity, but she soon acquired friends. Publicity stirred up by sympathizers such as James Boswell led to her receiving an unconditional pardon.

A great issue throughout the transportation era was convict labour. The system called for the assignation of convicts to free farmers as something approaching slaves. They were desperately needed, and were never in surplus. Conditions varied, but those assigned to cruel or thoughtless landowners might suffer extraordinary hardships. Hughes quotes the *Sydney Herald* complaining in 1826 of the 'all too prevalent custom' of a master goading an assigned man to insolence or violence, whereby he would end up with fifty lashes and an extension of his servitude. And it could be worse. A Mr Scott was 'a demon incarnate':

> He was in the habit of putting handcuffs, and leg-irons on [his workers], and throwing them into a dungeon on that estate, where they remained generally for three days without either meat or drink . . . [He] did not trouble to take his men to court, but sentenced them for the most trivial offence, and just as his caprice dictated, to carry logs of wood on their shoulders, on his own veranda, and under his eye; these logs weighed from 50 to 100 pounds.

Similarly, among the governors and other colonial bureaucrats could be found authentic sadists, along with hopeless timeservers and a few – a very few – sensible, well-meaning administrators. Major Joseph Foveaux made a name for himself on Norfolk Island as 'one of them hard and determined men who believe in the lash more than the Bible', as one convict put it; under his command a sentence of 200 lashes was called 'a feeler'. Still, there were good men who tried against soul-destroying odds to improve the lot of convicts and move towards the creation of a civilized society. Lachlan Macquarie put down the Rum Corps and tried to make sense of the colony's administration. Alexander Maconochie briefly instituted a humane regime on Norfolk Island. An ex-convict named William Redfern was responsible for introducing the first decent public health service. But nothing except time and the collapse of the system could really offer much hope.

Today, reading *The Fatal Shore*, it is difficult to believe that it could have been produced in anything less than a lifetime. In fact, it took Hughes under ten years, at a time when he was also art critic for *Time* magazine and writing other pieces. But he did have a personal commitment to his subject. He was born in Australia and was a member of that remarkable crew (together with Clive James and Germaine Greer) who brought their disruptive talents to Europe in the 1960s. He was clearly fascinated by his national heritage. What is amazing is that he could turn his hand from writing powerful art criticism (as in his classic *The Shock of the New*) to equally powerful and profound history. Besides, he could hardly be bettered as a phrase-maker. Who else would describe, with blinding accuracy, a Merino sheep as 'a pompous, ambling peruke' or comment that it was 'no wonder that the convicts pilfered like ants'?

Hughes, who died in 2012, has been criticized in Australia for concentrating too much on the dark side, the horrors, of the convict experience. Yet there is no question that those eighty years were full of the most appalling cruelty, and any attempt to minimize it would be dishonest. Moreover, *The Fatal Shore*, as Clive James has wisely remarked, is 'one of those rare achievements in the writing of history by which the unimaginably inhumane is brought to book without making us give up on humanity'. There was terrible pain in the founding of Australia; Hughes is right to make us feel it. We should be grateful that he does so in a book of such striking eloquence and readability.

As an editor CHARLES ELLIOTT published *The Fatal Shore* and other books by Robert Hughes, none of which required much editing.

Uncle Vanya Drops in

WILLIAM PALMER

A friend and neighbour died last year. Aged 100, he was a Pole who had fought in the war, spoke English and several other languages impeccably, and was both charming and tough-minded. He kept his powerful intellect almost until the end. I used to play chess with him once a week and only realized he was mortal when I unexpectedly beat him one afternoon. It wasn't until his late nineties that he became housebound and I then ran several curious errands for him.

At the age of 98 he wanted to brush up his Latin verb conjugations. I found him a copy of Kennedy's *Primer* in a shop in Charing Cross Road. Then he needed a new stem for his ancient pipe, from a shop, redolent with cigar fumes, in Jermyn Street. He continued smoking to the end. One day he asked me to get him some new flints for his petrol lighter. This was more difficult. The local supermarket was the source of his tobacco. I would try there. The young woman at the counter was puzzled. 'Flints,' I repeated. 'What are they?' 'You put them in a lighter,' I said. She looked as if she wanted to be somewhere else. 'We do have lighters,' she said. 'No,' I said, 'my friend has a lighter. He wants some flints.'

Each time I repeated the word, it seemed more outlandish. I steeled myself to explain that a flint was a small cylindrical piece of stone that was inserted in a hole at the top of the lighter. By depressing a lever, a ribbed metal wheel could be caused to rub against the flint, so creating a spark that set light to a petrol-soaked wick. Somehow I

Roy Lewis, *The Evolution Man, or How I Ate My Father* (1960), is out of print but we can obtain good second-hand copies.

couldn't rise to it. The world seemed to have advanced several decades in a few minutes.

When I reported back, my friend mused that technology might have advanced, but the use of flints to make fire was probably the last example of a technology we shared with people of the Stone Age. I should read *The Evolution Man*, he said. He would lend it to me.

I had never heard of its author, Roy Lewis, but pieced together some information about him. Born in 1913, educated at King Edward's School in Birmingham and University College, Oxford, Lewis spent much of his adult life as a journalist working for, among others, the *Economist* and *The Times*. He devoted his retirement to running his one-man-band publishing business, the Keepsake Press, producing mostly hand-printed pamphlets by poets; an admirable way to pass one's declining years and celebrated in his *The Practice of Parlour Printing considered as a Specific against Insomnia and Like Disorders with a warning on Side Effects*. In earlier years he had written several books on colonialism in Africa and other social and political issues, but of his three novels only *The Evolution Man* (1960) was a success.

The setting is southern Africa at the end of the Stone Age. Now, in the absence of any contemporaneous Stone Age literature we have to make do with what modern writers have imagined. William Golding's *The Inheritors* is probably the most famous example of the genre, although it holds to much the same line of monosyllabic conversation and names (Lok, Mal, Nil) as most other works set in prehistoric times. Golding's Neanderthals are gentle, dreamy, in tune with nature; noble savages who are no match for the extremely unpleasant *Homo sapiens* they encounter.

There is little of the noble savage in *The Evolution Man*. It was the comic genius of Roy Lewis to make his characters use urbane and anachronistic language, and to give each a perfectly sensible name. The narrator, Ernest, is a Stone Age boy of about 15. He lives in a cave, seized from a family of bears, with a largish horde of four brothers and five sisters, his parents and a number of husbandless aunts.

A fire is kept going almost continuously in the mouth of the cave, affording comfort and protection from the bears and other wild animals, though older and more conservative relatives, such as Uncle Vanya, have their doubts about this dangerous and unstable element:

When ground temperatures were low enough, or the dank rain closed in and made one's joints creak and ache, Uncle Vanya would come and visit. During a lull in the noise of the jungle traffic you would hear him coming, with a swish-swish-swish through the tree tops punctuated by an occasional ominous crack of an overburdened branch, and a muffled oath, which became a scream of uninhibited rage when he actually fell.

Uncle Vanya is old-school, arguing with Ernest's father about the unnatural and dangerous evil of fire, and the moral debilitation brought on by new ways of shaping flints and pebbles into weapons and tools.

The family have not yet made the connection between fire and cooking, and they continue to eat raw plants and meat. Ernest admits that their health and temper are constantly soured by gastric disturbances: 'the sunniest disposition is apt to be undermined by chronic colitis . . . Some fruits, some fungi, some roots could be eaten; others could not: pioneers all down the Stone Age had given their lives to discover which were which.'

Father worries endlessly that his horde is not evolving fast enough, but they are making some progress. One cold night when Uncle Vanya comes to call and sits in front of the detested fire, Ernest's younger half-brother Alexander makes an important discovery:

There, on the surface of the rock, was Uncle Vanya's shadow, faithfully outlined in charcoal . . . It was unmistakeably Uncle Vanya's shadow; nobody could mistake those huge bent shoulders, those hairy half-flexed knees and shaggy buttocks . . . that simian arm extended in a typical gesture of denunciation.

'What is it?' demanded Uncle Vanya in a terrible voice . . .

'Representational art,' squeaked Alexander.

Father's mind, however, is working on ever more ambitious schemes. He announces that his sons are to join him in an expedition. Now that they have reached puberty, he says, it is high time they find themselves mates. There is a horde a few miles away with girls of a marriageable age. They must each steal one away.

The boys protest that they have their own girls at home. Their sisters.

'People *always* mate with their sisters,' Oswald said. 'It's the done thing.'

'Not any more,' said Father. 'Exogamy begins right here. We must mix up the genes a bit . . . In short a young man must go out and find his mate, court her, capture her, fight for her . . . When you are all happily mated, you can bring the girls home.'

The girl picked by Ernest from this alien horde is not an easy catch. Her feet and her wits are considerably faster than his. She leads him a merry dance through savannah and swamp, across rivers and lakes, up and down mountains. At last, after days of pursuit, exhausted and disconsolate, Ernest blunders into a glade in the forest. And there she sits, on a fallen tree trunk,

casually combing her long tawny hair with the backbone of a fish . . . [She] smiled at me.

'You do look hot . . . and bothered.'

'I've got you now,' I said dispiritedly and raised my shillelagh.

She patted the tree trunk. 'Come and sit beside me and tell me all about yourself. I'm simply dying to know.'

So Ernest meets and falls in love with Griselda. His brothers have had equal luck with Clementina, Honoria and Petronella. After an idyllic period of courtship, the boys make their way home with their new mates.

Meanwhile, Father has been getting on with evolution. He has discovered the delight of cooked meat, and how to make fire without having to climb the volcano. There is a slight setback when he sets the surrounding jungle alight but, in bartering for new caves and land with an already resident horde, he invents modern diplomacy. Other ideas, however, prove to be altogether too much for his conservative sons, and he suffers the fate of many visionary pioneers – of being destroyed by the less enlightened.

In this wonderfully entertaining and witty book the how and the why of the evolution of our early ancestors is telescoped into the history of a single horde of cave-dwellers. It is clear the improvements and discoveries are mostly down to one man, and how far other members of the horde would have progressed without the intellectual push of Father is a moot point.

The Stone Age came to an end 8,000 years ago, but it's not so difficult to imagine Ernest and his family living in a large Victorian rectory with little change in their language or basic thought processes. After all, 8,000 years might seem a long time ago, but it appears a bit closer when you realize it represents only eighty generations of sturdy and clever centenarians like my good Polish friend. I can imagine his forebears doing interesting things with flints.

WILLIAM PALMER's collection of poems, *The Water Steps*, was published by Rack Press in 2017. His seventh novel, *The Devil Is White*, was published by Jonathan Cape in 2013. He is very glad to have at last exceeded the number produced by Jane Austen and E. M. Forster.

Not Your Average Englishwoman

JUSTIN MAROZZI

I first encountered Rosita Forbes atop a camel in the middle of the Rabiana Sand Sea in southern Libya. There was probably no finer way of making this unusual writer's acquaintance. Here, deep in the Sahara, she was in her element, disguised as an Arab woman and with only a few camels and human companions between her and a nasty, lingering death. In fact it was worse than that. Apart from the natural dangers of the desert, she was passing through the territory of tribesmen who regarded this motley expedition of an Englishwoman and the Egyptian Olympic-fencer-cum-spy-cum-explorer Ahmed Hassanein Bey with profound suspicion, if not downright hostility.

'We posted sentinels at night, slept with our revolvers cocked beside us and by day went armed with such an array of weapons that the hostile Zouiya villagers decided we were better left alone,' she wrote in *The Secret of the Sahara: Kufara* (1921). It was just as well they took such precautions. On leaving the entrancing oasis of Buzeima, she overheard a Zwaya tribesman mutter bitterly: 'You should not escape thus; we had men enough to kill you.'

Rosita Forbes was not your average Englishwoman. Born in 1890, the daughter of a Lincolnshire squire and MP, she refused to settle for the traditional role expected of her. In an era of travel and exploration dominated by the tweedy gentlemen amateurs of the Royal Geographical Society, she held her own and bowed to no man. Beautiful, flamboyant and independent, she left school at 17, married

---

Rosita Forbes, *The Secret of the Sahara: Kufara* (1921), is available as a print-on-demand paperback. We can also obtain good second-hand hardback copies.

a colonel at 21 and then during the First
World War spent two years as an ambu-
lance driver on the Western Front, win-
ning two medals from the French government. She divorced her first colonel in
1917 (pawning her wedding ring to fund
an unsuccessful expedition home on horse-
back from Durban) and married her second in 1921, a more successful union that
lasted until his death four decades later.

Pictures of Forbes in the 1920s show a
woman at the peak of her good looks, dressed in an array of party
ensembles and wide-brimmed hats of varying extravagance. In one she
stares down the barrels of a shotgun at the onlooker, head cocked
beneath a raffish fedora, one eye closed, the other eyeing her target
with a cool, unflustered eye. In another, at the Jewels of Empire Ball at
Brook House on Park Lane in 1930, she sports a pearl sautoir that
tumbles down the plunging neckline of a velvet ballgown and an
astonishingly exuberant ostrich feather and diamanté headdress.

So much for Rosita Forbes at play. From childhood she was capti-
vated by stories of travel. 'I always collected maps,' she wrote in
Adventure, an early memoir published in 1928.

> The curly red lines across African deserts had the fascination of
> a magnet, and I hoped fervently that the pioneers who were
> writing their names over the blank spaces would leave just one
> small desert for me.

They did. It was a patch of the Libyan Sahara, which she explored
with Ahmed Hassanein Bey in 1920–1 and wrote about in perhaps
her finest book. *The Secret of the Sahara* is the high-spirited story of
this expedition to the remote oasis of Kufra, which she was only the
second European to see. Their route lay through the famous oasis of

Buzeima, a sapphire cleft in the sand-blown desert, and home, so she was warned, to 'a particularly savage portion of the Zouiya tribe . . . [who] attacked every strange caravan at sight'.

I remember reading Forbes's extraordinarily evocative description of the desert around Buzeima as I approached it on the back of my own faithful camel. It was a savage arena of black mountain ridges, towering cliffs of Nubian sandstone, dark despite the dazzle of the sun, lying like shattered cathedrals hurled across a sandy, flint-strewn plain. At once awful and uplifting, it struck Forbes as 'a veritable inferno of desolation'. After this harsh introduction, the oasis seemed like paradise.

> Buzeima is the loveliest oasis I have ever seen, with its strange ruddy hills – jewels purple and crimson reflected in the silver salt mirage which girdles the bluest lake in the world. All this colour is clear cut against the soft, pale dunes. It is seen through a frame of drooping palm branches with perhaps a rose-hued figure, scarlet sashed, guarding a flock of goats by a dark pool among high green rushes.

Kufra was the climax of the expedition, reached only after overcoming the challenges of treacherous tribesmen, suffocating sandstorms and ailing camels. She confesses to having become obsessed with this holy oasis: 'nucleus of the greatest Islamic confraternity rigidly guarded from every stranger, the centre of the mighty influence against which every European Power has battled in turn, [it] stirred my imagination'. Nor did it disappoint. She found its setting magical, fringed by hills glowing mauve and violet at sunset, the fading emerald and sapphire of date palm and lake half aflame among the burning sands.

Her first-hand account of Jaghbub, another isolated oasis town virtually impenetrable to foreigners, was the highlight of the return journey north. Seat of the ascetic Sanusi Order, a fiercely orthodox Sufi Islamic revivalist movement, Jaghbub boasted the Zawia, or religious lodge, which by the late nineteenth century was Africa's second greatest university, after Cairo's Al Azhar. The Sanusis led the indigenous resistance to brutal colonial occupation by fascist Italy. After their battlefield heroics, they were ultimately crushed by the Italians who rounded up the population of Cyrenaica (eastern Libya) into mass concentration camps, poisoned wells and sent men to die a slow death in the salt pans. The Italians captured and executed the Sanusi leader Omar al Mukhtar in 1931 after a show trial lasting only minutes. (Colonel Gaddafi piled further humiliations on the Sanusi family and their followers, hounding relatives into exile after he toppled the Sanusi monarchy of King Idris in 1969 and razing the noble Zawia to the ground in 1988.)

Every desert traveller faces a reckoning at the end of a long journey. 'I lay on my back and looked at the stars, weighing the balance of success and failure and, suddenly, I felt that this was not really the end,' Forbes wrote. 'Some time, somehow, I knew not where or when, but most assuredly when Allah willed, I should come back to the deserts and the strange, uncharted tracks would bear my camels south again.'

She never did, but still there was no end to her travels elsewhere. Gertrude Bell may have damned her with a spiteful, unsisterly flourish – 'in the matter of trumpet-blowing she is unique' – but this did not prevent Forbes from becoming a celebrity travel writer who was in demand on both sides of the Atlantic. It is true that Forbes was never backward in coming forward – in *The Secret of the Sahara* the second photo shows 'The author as a Beduin Sheikh', and the Arabic-speaking, desert-navigating Egyptian, without whom she might well not have survived, is controversially rather written out of the story. But to accuse a travel writer of self-promotion is like complaining about an English batting collapse. Some things in life are inevitable. Besides, male travel writers and explorers were just the same – no one would ever have considered Richard Burton a shrinking violet. In Libya Forbes had won her spurs, the cue for a royal audience at Buckingham Palace and a fellowship of the Royal Geographical

Society. As for her book, serialized in the *Sunday Times*, it was a runaway success.

More, perhaps too many, followed, including a dozen forgotten and forgettable romantic novels. Her travel writing was of a higher order and reflected her unstoppable zest for travel to some of the world's most difficult and dangerous places. From the Middle East and Africa in the 1920s, she moved on to Central Asia, Eastern Europe and the Soviet Union, then South America and the Caribbean in the 1930s.

If maps were magnetic for Forbes, powerful men were irresistible to this dashing society beauty. Although she lacked a university degree, unlike Gertrude Bell and Freya Stark, and was told by a *Telegraph* executive that she was far too pretty to get on as a foreign correspondent ('As long as you look like that, you haven't a chance to be taken seriously'), she made her own way, interviewing statesmen around the world. Her circle of friends and acquaintances included kings (Iraq, Greece, Bulgaria) and queens (England, Romania), aristocrats, politicians and celebrities. It was a lasting regret that her services were never called upon by the wartime British government, again unlike those of her contemporaries Bell and Stark.

Yet perhaps the interview in a rose garden with Hitler and the flirtation with Benito Mussolini were an adventure too far. Though she protested that they were no more than journalistic interviews, the timing of their publication in *These Men I Knew* (1940), in which Stalin, Goebbels and King Zog also featured, was inauspicious. After the war she and her husband retired to their own private Eden on a 400-acre estate in the Bahamas. The writing dried up a couple of books later and, after a glamorous, hard-won career forged simultaneously on the road less travelled and in England's society pages, Rosita Forbes retreated into the oblivion that awaits us all.

Like Rosita Forbes, JUSTIN MAROZZI hopes 'the strange, uncharted tracks' of the Sahara will one day bear his camels south again.

Haikus among the Pears

OLIVIA POTTS

A Jane Grigson quotation sits on my desk. It's written on a scrappy Post-it note; the glue on the back has picked up dust and a stray piece of cotton. It wasn't meant to become a permanent feature, rather a scribble to remind myself to write the line somewhere more lasting, but I can't quite bring myself to throw it away. It reads: 'Anyone who likes to eat, can soon learn to cook well.' It embodies Jane Grigson's approach to food, pulling the rug from under those who shroud cooking in mystery or snobbery. For someone like me, who came to cooking relatively late in life, it is a mantra to live by. Grigson was a cook who, above all, loved to eat. Eating well is both the starting point and the ultimate end of all her cookery writing – as it surely should be for all cooking.

Jane Grigson was never quite as famous as her contemporary and friend Elizabeth David, but she is the cook's cook. Her cookery was firmly grounded in her kitchen – whether in her English home in Wiltshire or her French home in the Loire valley. Her recipes weren't as exotic as David's, though the ingredients were sometimes unfamiliar. They were less about introducing readers to new cuisines than coaxing them towards a better kind of home cooking. And every recipe was infused with her characteristic wit and knowledge; where

---

Jane Grigson's Fruit Book (1982) is available as a print-on-demand edition. We can also obtain second-hand copies of the original edition.

David's writing tends towards the arch, Grigson's exudes warmth.

She fell into food writing by accident. After a holiday in France, she and her husband, the poet and critic Geoffrey Grigson, along with their young daughter Sophie, bought a house in Troo in the Loire valley. She was immediately smitten with the French approach to food. While there she became interested in charcuterie and the preparation of meat, and suggested to a friend that he write a book about it. But after he bailed out of the project, Grigson was asked to see it through. The result was her first book, *Charcuterie and French Pork Cookery* (1967), a comprehensive and ground-breaking work, unlike anything that had come before.

Following its success, Elizabeth David recommended Grigson to the *Observer* as a food columnist. By her own admission, she felt out of her depth, but she approached it as she had the charcuterie book (and would go on to approach all future food writing projects): she took a topic and researched it exhaustively. She continued the column until her death twenty-two years later, and other books followed, all approached with her usual rigour.

Jane Grigson's Fruit Book, published in 1982, was her last, and is my favourite. The *Fruit Book* demonstrates what Grigson is best at: down-to-earth treatment of a broad topic, peppered with humour, stories and scholarship. It is, as the title suggests, a comprehensive book of fruit cookery, taking the reader from apples to watermelon via Cornelian cherries and loquats, figs and strawberries. It would be an ambitious book if written today, but for the early 1980s it was unprecedented. Loquats are hard to come by now; back then, they sounded like something you might find on the moon.

Grigson's style effortlessly mixes the scholarly and the literary with the practical and the personal, and nowhere more enjoyably than in the *Fruit Book*. Haikus are sprinkled among the pears, Bermudan verse opens the papaya chapter, descriptions of the plum in art and literature are followed by an anecdote about aphrodisiacs, and horticultural details about each fruit's cultivation are woven in with the recipes.

Another of the joys of Grigson is her humour. Sometimes it tends towards the bawdy and even the scatological, but it is her gentle, wry observations that I love most:

> My feeling towards dried figs is ambivalent – they remind me of the syrup of figs I once spat out on the nursery carpet and all over a blue dressing-gown. It must be the smell . . . One member of the family eats a dried fig every night before he goes to bed. This is a ritual I have come to admire, since tackling dried figs for this book.

She can always be relied on for the perfect opening line. Whether she is writing about sorb apples ('We were sitting in a large garden, our feet in cool grass, watching Russian dancers'), or common-or-garden apples ('The apple was the first fruit of the world, according to Genesis, but it was no Cox's orange pippin. God gave the crab apple, and left the rest to Man.'), her chapter openings cannot fail to draw you in. But she is never pretentious. The mulberry chapter begins, simply: 'Four things I like about the mulberry'.

Her descriptions are enticing. Of gooseberries, she asks: 'When Constable painted and drew elder bushes in flower, creamy panicles tilted against green, I wonder if he had ever tasted their muscat sweetness with gooseberries? Lyrical painting we have been good at, lyrical cooking has been rare with us.' Lyrical cooking may still be rare, but this is lyrical cookery writing.

It is impossible simply to flick through the *Fruit Book*: it is too persuasive. Time and again, as I reread it, I find myself breaking off and padding into the kitchen, abandoning whatever it was I was meant to be doing to follow Grigson's suggestion that I try stuffing apples with zest and nuts, or wondering how long it would take me to knock up a Spanish fig ice cream.

For the inexperienced cook, she can be intimidating. She often assumes much more of the reader than modern publishers would allow: 'You do not need instruction in making little sweet shortcrust boats,' she says confidently, while I – a trained pastry chef – wonder idly how one even begins. Frequently, she gives no quantities beyond something like 'equal weights of strawberries and raspberries'; many of her recipes use ratios rather than exact quantities.

But perhaps, with the exception of shortcrust boats, this makes perfect sense. So much of cooking relies on sense and senses, on taste and tasting. Grigson trusts her readers to use their judgement. She knows that cookery is not a one-size-fits-all activity; that ripeness and provenance determine the power of any given fruit; that some prefer their raspberry fools thick, and some thin. She's there by your side, holding your hand for soufflés and mayonnaise. She won't leave you in the lurch when something might impair a dish. But when it comes to matters of taste or availability, she trusts you.

Oddly, some of my favourite bits of Grigson are about foods she *doesn't* like. In the *Fruit Book*, rhubarb receives the full force of her scorn:

Nanny-food. Governess-food. School-meal-food (cold porridge with rhubarb for breakfast). And I haven't got over disliking rhubarb, and disliking it still more for being often not so young and a little stringy. Also rhubarb's country of origin is Siberia. Stewed rhubarb with frozen mammoth?

But luckily for those of us who don't share her view, she still gives half a dozen recipes for the stuff.

Of course she's not infallible. I'm ready to give her lemon sandwiches a miss (a brief hope that this was an unassuming title for something delicious was scotched on reading the recipe: it is literally raw lemons, sliced and placed between bread and butter). On other occasions she requires more of the reader than perhaps they are willing to give. I spot a recipe named simply 'peaches on toast', but balk at the first nonchalant instruction: 'the first thing to think about is the bread. If you cannot buy a brioche loaf, or good white milk bread, you must make your own.' I won't. I imagine few will. But her brilliance – her clarity of writing, her strikingly straightforward recipes, her naked love for food in all its forms – makes you forgive her excesses.

Jane Grigson died on 12 March 1990. In her obituary, Alan Davidson described her as 'the most companionable presence in the kitchen'. It is for this and for the generosity of her writing that she is loved. There are a lot of food writers I admire, a whole host I respect, there are some I even feel I know. But it's Jane who I want as my friend, her kitchen that I want to sit in, her cooking I want to watch.

OLIVIA POTTS is a writer and chef. She practised as a criminal barrister before retraining in patisserie at Le Cordon Bleu. Her first book, *A Half Baked Idea*, a memoir about love, grief and cake, will be published by Fig Tree this July.

The wood engravings in this article are by Clare Leighton and are taken from her *Four Hedges* (1935).

An Incurable Topophilia

ANDREW NIXON

When I was a boy in the early 1980s the most thrilling place on earth was the local shopping centre car park.

Picture me, all agog in the back seat as my father fearlessly pilots our Ford Cortina into a mind-bending maze of grey concrete, up through weird spiralling tunnels and geometric caves which become darker and danker the higher we go, giving the curious sensation of ascending into a pit. This place is from the future, yet it is decaying. Litter rustles in cold corners. Stalactites drip from ledges. Damp oozes from the concrete's very pores. And then suddenly we emerge into a sunlit Dan Dare roofscape of giant corkscrew-shaped ramps, cubist columns and obscurely hostile watchtowers.

This was the Tricorn Centre, Portsmouth. I was much puzzled by

Jonathan Meades, *Museum without Walls* (2012) · Unbound · Pb · 464pp · £10.99 · ISBN 9781783520190; and *An Encyclopaedia of Myself* (2014) · 4th Estate · Pb · 352pp · £10.99 · ISBN 9781857029055. *Filthy English* (1984), *Peter Knows What Dick Likes* (1989) and *Pompey* (1993) are out of print.

it. Why was it so disorienting, so ungraspable in its geography? Why was it so jarringly different from all the other places I was taken to? It frightened and fascinated me. But it never occurred to me to *despise* it. Only much later did I learn that that was what you were supposed to do, that the Tricorn was the ultimate 1960s Concrete Monstrosity, abhorred by all decent folk and derided by Prince Charles as 'a mildewed lump of elephant droppings'.

When the city council ordered it to be torn down in 2004 crowds gathered to cheer. But I didn't, and neither did Jonathan Meades. He said: 'You don't go knocking down Stonehenge or Lincoln Cathedral. Buildings like the Tricorn were as good as that. They were great monuments of an age.' And that is just one among many reasons why I think Meades is the most outrageously interesting writer about British places alive today and possibly ever.

Jonathan Turner Meades (born 1947) is perhaps best known for his television programmes in which he ambles around sheds, dockyards and concrete monstrosities making gnomic, swallowed-a-thesaurus pronouncements while dressed like one of the Blues Brothers. He has somehow managed to make over fifty such programmes for the BBC, despite paying no attention whatsoever to the accepted rules of mainstream broadcasting. His modus operandi is to craft the scripts first, then report to the director on filming day and simply act them out. The words always take precedence, which is why the likes of *Abroad in Britain* (1990) and *Magnetic North* (2008) are funny and intellectually invigorating but so uncompromisingly wordy that they can only be understood after multiple rewatchings with a good dictionary to hand. For Meades is not a 'television presenter' at all, but rather an author who occasionally makes television programmes. His considerable written oeuvre includes fiction, memoir, reportage, cultural history, literary criticism and even a highly idiosyncratic cookbook. His specialist subject, however, is *place*.

'Place' isn't architecture, though Meades is certainly expert on that. Place includes buildings but also the gaps between them and the

B-roads that lead to them. It encompasses 'deserted streets, seething boulevards, teeming beaches, empty steppes, black reservoirs, fields of agricultural scrap, cute villages and disappearing points which have an unparalleled capacity to promote hope'. Place surrounds us and is, he claims, the greatest free show on earth – hence the title of the book that collects his best writing on the topic: *Museum without Walls* (2012).

Its dust jacket carries his credo in capital letters: 'THERE IS NO SUCH THING AS A BORING PLACE'. Inside are erudite musings and unpredictable polemics on everything from St Paul's Cathedral to Birmingham's multi-storey car parks. Like Flaubert or Andy Warhol, Meades believes that everything is interesting if you bother to look at it for long enough, that 'the banal is a thing of joy'.

Not that he is uncritically appreciative of all he surveys. Goodness me, no – a more scathing, vituperative critic of architecture or indeed anything else you will struggle to find. In fact his capacity for hatred is legendary. But to properly hate something you have to be interested in it, and Meades is interested in bad architecture, and in what makes it bad ('the catastrophic cock-ups of grandiloquent visionaries are as grimly appealing as the imaginatively bereft efforts of volume builders'). He is particularly contemptuous of the 'aesthetic tyranny' of the National Trust and English Heritage, who hold that only the naturally picturesque is worthy of contemplation. Meades observes that the fields, woods and waterways of the British countryside are no more 'natural' than skyscrapers or scrapyards. All are products of man's intervention, all carry a story or foment an idea in the viewer if only he has eyes to see. Everything that's been put somewhere tells you something about the people who did the putting. So he extends the courtesy of close attention and appreciation to the 'ugly and dreary' bits of the great Museum without Walls, to 'heaths, chance conjunctions, field systems, wide verges, sunken lanes, hidden alleys, high roads and the nameless bits between them all. Especially those bits.'

Meades contracted his 'incurable topophilia' in childhood. His father 'travelled in biscuits': he was a sales rep for Crawfords and would take his son along in the company Morris 8 on his rounds in Wiltshire and neighbouring counties. While Meades senior sold custard creams to corner shops, Meades junior was free to wander the streets of Winchester or Shaftesbury unaccompanied, observing and absorbing. He peered through hedges, read billboards, noticed things. He taught himself odd tricks, like how to tell where he was 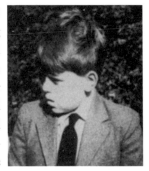 by the composition of the roadside walls (south of Salisbury Plain they're chequered patterns of flint and stone, whereas in Hampshire the flint is laid in alternating rows with brick, apparently). He diligently made maps of his voyages: naïve and inaccurate, of course, but reflective of the child's attempt to make sense of the world.

This self-education formed him. He learnt about buildings without the filter of received wisdom and so remained ignorant of 'aesthetic hierarchies'. No adult taught him that 'stone is nobler than brick, that brick is nobler than pebbledash, that pebbledash is nobler than breezeblock, that breezeblock is nobler than corrugated iron'. He wasn't told that churches are axiomatically superior to pubs, nor that original Tudor houses must be better than the 1920s mock variety.

He did have architectural epiphanies. A school cricket match took him to Marsh Court, a deliriously complex building by Edwin Lutyens which he experienced as a 'dream house', meaning that it seemed to transform itself as he walked around it and had the 'logic and movement and seamless metamorphoses that characterize dreams'. But for the most part he just ambled slowly about in ordinary places, staring upwards, mouth open, making his own judgements. He's been doing more or less the same thing ever since.

The formative places and people of Meades's provincial 1950s childhood are depicted in glorious technicolour in *An Encyclopaedia of Myself* (2014). This disordered memoir – brimful of bogus Majors, grasping relatives and other top-notch English eccentrics – is his warmest and most purely enjoyable book. Otherwise, 'warm enjoyment' is not quite the typical Jonathan Meades reading experience. His style is bracing, abrasive, combative. His prose fizzes like acid added to a test tube of chalk. He is master of both the pithy one-line put-down and the extended digression that yanks you out of a thought, whizzes you through a bewildering Tricorn Centre of surprise analogies and uncomfortable truths, then dumps you back down again with preconceptions shattered and a disconcerting sense of the scale of your own ignorance. By refusing to talk down to the reader while disdainfully denigrating all the things you happen to believe, Meades has a rare way of making you feel clever and stupid at the same time. And he is a self-described prose maximalist – after all, why merely skewer a misconception when you can bury it under an avalanche of difficult synonyms?

Meades sharpened his critical skills during a fifteen-year stint as *The Times*'s restaurant critic, where he was noted for proffering very strong, very well-informed opinions on everything, sometimes even the food. Absolute creative freedom is a given for Meades. He is one of those fortunate Baby Boomers who seemed to be in the right place (London) at the right time (the late 1960s) to carve out a career in following successive whims. His first writing job was for *Books and Bookmen*, a now-defunct literary magazine which gave him licence to report on whatever took his fancy – thus, discourses on topics ranging from Parisian transsexuals to Jorge Luis Borges can be found in the superb compilation *Peter Knows What Dick Likes* (1989).

His fiction, meanwhile, is designed to shock. The short stories in *Filthy English* (1984) apply highfalutin' linguistic virtuosity to scabrous subject-matter, including incest and worse. The wilfully repellent novel *Pompey* (1993) has been described as a masterpiece by some – eliciting comparisons with Joyce, Swift and Sterne – and dismissed as unreadable by others. I suppose I have a foot in both camps: I think it's a virtually unreadable masterpiece.

As a writer on place he is even harder to pigeonhole. Perhaps if he were French he would seem less of an eccentric outlier. Indeed, the country that gave the world such concepts as the *flâneur* and the *lieu de mémoire* is his adopted home. But he is also an extremely *English* writer, who returns again and again to dig under the skin of his homeland. Stephen Fry claimed that 'no one understands England better' and I suspect that Meades's obsession with English urban decay and rural squalor is actually a perverse form of patriotism. He admires John Betjeman and the largely forgotten architectural critic Ian Nairn, both of whom urged us to notice the ordinary, the sub-urban, the industrial. But Meades has taken the idea that there is no such thing as a boring place so much further than they did, and – along with his more poetically minded contemporary Iain Sinclair – has in turn inspired a generation of rather self-conscious 'psycho-geographers' who can't pass a rusty shed or shopping trolley-filled canal without penning a woozy meditation.

Yet there is nothing affected about Meades's extreme topophilia. That's why it's contagious, why reading him has changed how I try to look at the world. He really does love B-road laybys and naval dry-dock facilities and, yes, certain brutalist concrete buildings. So when he described the Tricorn Centre in Portsmouth as one of 'the most thrilling works to have been made in Britain' and 'a great monument to an age' like Lincoln Cathedral, he wasn't merely being provocative or contrarian, he meant it.

The Tricorn was designed by a prodigiously talented British archi-tect named Rodney Gordon. Gordon's work wasn't pretty or easy on the eye but it was striking, original, clever and challenging. It was *difficult*. But then so is *Hamlet*, so is *Ulysses*, so is Picasso's *Guernica*. As Jonathan Meades himself asks, why shouldn't our buildings some-times be a bit difficult – like the best novels or plays or paintings? Or, indeed, like the best critics.

ANDREW NIXON is a writer and co-founder of The Dabbler blog. He has met Meades several times and found him to be an absolute pussycat – honestly.

A Burning Issue

PIERS PLOWRIGHT

This is the tale of a baby, a book and a candle. The setting is the Sudan, the baby is our first-born, two-month-old Natasha, and the book is a great twentieth-century Italian novel. As for the candle . . .

One may as well begin with the baby.

Natasha Su-ming Sakina Plowright was born on 22 February 1966 in Omdurman, a stone's throw from the Mahdi's tomb, to my wife Poh Sim and me. She weighed 8lbs 6oz and was bright blue. Her nearest neighbour in the nun-run hospital was a Greek grocer's baby weighing in at over 10lbs. We carried ours home in triumph and a Moses basket to our eccentric, edge-of-desert house, set in a garden full of mongooses.

I was working in the Sudan for the British Council, and Poh Sim, born in Malaya, had interrupted her M.Phil. on John Ford – the playwright, not the movie-maker – to join me. We'd been married eighteen months. Her reading taste was far wider and deeper than mine and among the writers she introduced me to were W. B. Yeats, whom I'd never read, and the Italian novelist Cesare Pavese, whom I'd never heard of. The novel that really spoke to her was his last, *La Luna e i falò* (*The Moon and the Bonfires*), written in 1949. It's a powerful tale of the return of an Italian American who's made good to the remote Italian village where he grew up before the Second World War. You never know the narrator's name but you get to know everybody else in that small place intimately, particularly his old friend

---

Cesare Pavese, *The Moon and the Bonfires* (1949) · Trans. R. W. Flint
New York Review of Books · Pb · 176pp · £14.95 · ISBN 9781590170212

Nuto, a Zorba-like figure, exemplifying courage and freethinking in the otherwise narrow and cruel society they've both grown up in. Gradually, terrible events unfold, and always there's that sense of the secret which, for me, marks out great fiction. Italo Calvino expressed this perfectly when he wrote: 'Each one of Pavese's novels revolves around a hidden theme, something unsaid which is the real thing he wants to say and which can be expressed only by not mentioning it.'

What gives this one an extra punch is something Pavese definitely didn't mention: that he was at the end of his tether after a broken love affair and had already stockpiled the sleeping pills with which he would kill himself five months after finishing the novel.

Poh Sim had been telling me about *The Moon and the Bonfires* shortly before Natasha was born and I wanted to read it. But she'd left her copy in Kuala Lumpur and there were none in the bookshops of Khartoum. And then at some embassy do I sat next to the learned, and – as it turned out – fastidious, wife of a Second Secretary and we got talking about books. Yes of course she'd read Pavese and actually she had a copy of *The M&Bs* sitting on her bookshelves only a few streets away. Could I . . . ? I *could*, provided I was immensely careful with it and returned it promptly. We might even have an in-depth discussion one evening.

So the next day I brought it home, a slim paperback, with a bright red moon and a golden bonfire on the front cover. And began to read. And was hooked. And then Natasha arrived.

She was a restive baby and we had no idea what to do about it or how to keep her cool at night. We tried putting her on the veranda just outside our open-shuttered window with wire netting round her. Because of the mongooses that sometimes ate more than snakes. But she didn't like it there so we brought her cot inside, next to our bed, under the water-cooler and that was better. *Provided* we didn't switch any lights on. And this is where the candle comes in.

Natasha seemed to find candlelight soothing and I liked reading by it, just before I fell asleep. I must have got about halfway through

Pavese's masterpiece when, one particularly hot evening, Poh Sim and Natasha asleep beside me, I joined them, the book still in my hand and the bedside candle still burning.

I don't know who woke first, but it was to a small conflagration. The flame had caught the book which had fallen to the floor, the moon was being devoured by the bonfire, and the edges of the rush bedside mat had caught fire. We leapt out of bed, stamped on the candle, book and mat, and put the fire out before, amazingly, Natasha woke. The humans were safe but literature wasn't.

And what to do about the wife of the Second Secretary who would not, we thought, be amused. A plan was hatched: a London pianist was due to give a concert in Khartoum in a month's time under the auspices of the British Council. If we could track down a copy of the same edition of the Pavese in Foyles – was it still in print? – and get it to the pianist whom I vaguely knew, he could bring it with him, sandwiched between music scores and cigars, and we could gently hand it over as if it were the 'original'. Luckily there had been no signature or Ex Libris in that, and it had been in pristine condition. Well, a copy was found, the pianist was willing – all seemed well.

But then the enquiries began. She'd very much like the book back as she needed to refer to it urgently. Surely I must have finished it. Give me another week, I said. She did. Well, could she have it? It's somewhere in the house, I said – you know how untidy we are. Just give me a few more days. She did. Well, had we found it? Not quite, I said. Well it must be somewhere, she said, I'll come over and look myself. Better not, I said, Natasha is still very wary of strangers and . . . Oh for heaven's sake, she said. And then, by God or embassy duties she was distracted, and the pianist flew in, the concert was a success, and the book was handed over.

I *did* eventually tell the Embassy wife: to her great credit she laughed, and we remained friends. But I never finished *The Moon and the Bonfires*. Until the other day when I found a new translation in our local bookshop. Another paperback with a haunting close-up photo on the front of children in shadow behind a crackling bonfire. I went back to the beginning and was spellbound as before. But this time – I was 28 then, I'm 80 now – it seemed much less a piece of history. The fascism that Pavese wrote about has returned to Italy, and hostility to those outside the local community is back with a vengeance. And the meaning of that moon and those bonfires has changed – dangerously so.

And, by the way, if you're worried about the baby, she stopped being blue after a few hours, has grown up wonderfully, and loves books.

After the British Council, PIERS PLOWRIGHT worked for BBC Radio and Poh Sim taught at Royal Holloway College. Natasha is now Head of Communications at the Photographers' Gallery in London.

Small Is Beautiful

MATT COLLINS

Among the books I'd assembled to help steer me through the boundless subject of trees and wood-lands for a recent commission, H. E. Bates's *Through the Woods* – a month-by-month account of a small copse in Kent – looked unassuming. Recommended via some unnerving algorithm of online commerce, it sat for many weeks among the accumulating pile beneath my desk. When at last I glanced through it, however, one passage brought it suddenly alive:

> Fear begins to come more quickly in a wood, with darkness and twilight, than in any other place I know. I have been in a wood gathering violets or orchis or primroses in the late evening, when the sudden realization of twilight coming down has sent a sudden damnable running of cold up my spine, and I have half run out of the place. That feeling is common.

When I later spent a long winter's night in the notoriously 'haunted' Wayland Wood in Norfolk, Bates tramped with me, not only helping me interpret the experience but also contributing to it an element of purposeful enquiry. 'A wood at night can be a strange place,' he writes. 'Why is it? It is not simply darkness. We grow used to darkness. It can only be some quality in trees themselves.'

In writing my own book, I was greatly helped by the observa-

H. E. Bates, *Through the Woods* (1936) · Illus. Agnes Miller Parker
Little Toller · Pb · 144pp · £12 · ISBN 9781908213020

tions of other writers. Some, like John Stewart Collis on his Dorset ash wood, and Roger Deakin on his global excursions from Suffolk, could always be relied on. Others kept me company on particular woodland jaunts: Jim Crumley in a Caledonian pine forest, Francis Parkman through strange tree farms on the North American prairie, Gertrude Jekyll, a little unexpectedly, on a wooded mountainside in Switzerland. But it was Bates's *Through the Woods* that became my constant companion.

His lyrical yet down-to-earth reflections upon the life of a little wood – a chestnut copse just outside the village of Little Chart Forstal in Kent, where he spent the greater part of his adult life – were ones I could always relate to. Like the very best nature writing they highlighted the remarkable within the unremarkable, the uncommon buried beneath the common, weaving the many different elements of a wood into an engaging, spirited narrative. *Through the Woods* is a book I wanted to quote from to the point of plagiarism: the best nature writing, I would argue, is often produced by novelists.

For most of us, woods, forests – a mere grouping of trees even – carry both a material presence and its immaterial shadow. Heightened by our natural responses to uncertainty, threat and enclosure, our senses all too readily weave a layer of fantasy into the physical fabric of a wood. As Bates himself puts it, 'There is some precious quality brought about by the close gathering together of trees into a wood that defies analysis.' As a novelist whose many stories inhabit the tall trunks and dark dells of a wood, he instinctively imbues his non-fiction account with the truth of human experience.

Herbert Ernest Bates was a prolific writer, producing 50 or so books in just over 50 years, most of them set in the English countryside and less than a third of them non-fiction. *Through the Woods*, one of his earliest, can be seen as a kind of behind-the-scenes tour of the stage on which so much of his life's work would be set, a methodical exercise in the lyrical observation of landscape that would form the bedrock of his fiction. Take, for instance, his description of the nightingale's song, pouring in early summer from the high woodland canopy, 'a performance made up, very often, more of silence than of utterance. The very silences have a kind of passion in them, a sense of breathlessness and restraint, of restraint about to be magically broken.'

The silences, he notes, are often broken by a long, protracted whistling, prolonged by the bird seemingly for pure enjoyment. These observations later turned up in the pages of his novella *The Triple Echo*, heightening a moment of romantic tension:

> Up in the beech trees the nightingale held to one long pure sustained high note. The soldier drew in his breath and held it too . . .
> 'Listen,' he said, 'listen to that.'
> Once again, together, they listened to the nightingale. Sometimes there were soundless, breathless pauses in the song.

Through the Woods was published in 1936, with beautiful wood engravings by Agnes Miller Parker. Bates was only 30 at the time and had yet to produce the books that cemented his literary career: *Fair Stood the Wind for France, Love for Lydia, The Darling Buds of May*, among many others. The woodland that became his muse for *Through the Woods* had only recently entered his life with his move to rural Kent, after marrying his childhood sweetheart and committing himself to writing. For him it was a kind of extension of the woods of his Northamptonshire childhood, which had provided an idyllic contrast to the unromantic reality of the factory work and stringent religious upbringing that had overshadowed his twenties.

So the wood at Little Chart Forstal was a portal to his happiest countryside memories and a place in which to stimulate them. 'The wood is not far from the house,' he begins: 'You can see it, in fact, from the windows. We might as well go straight down to it.' Beginning and ending in the month of April, Bates takes us on a meandering walking tour through the cycle of the seasons: we pass the opening of early flowers, the fruiting of coppiced chestnuts, the snows of winter.

The wind does not trouble us at all. It makes an incessant

swishing in the pines overhead . . . a whining, melancholy noise, and yet in some way sweet. We walk in stillness, in a primrose world of absolute spring.

He evokes the essence of his wood so well that visiting it, as I did one August morning last year, seemed to add little that I had not already experienced through his writing. It is his storyteller's voice and grasp of drama, revealed again and again in his various woodland encounters, that holds one's attention: foxes are 'tireless in their own devilries', wild cherry blooms are like 'columns of shining smoke'; the stillness of the wood itself is 'an expansive hush without wind, the strange silence of a small and confined world'. Bates even throws into this world a villain, the gamekeeper, universally loathed by the nature writer and very personally by Bates.

> You must not step an inch away from the path; you must not look at a pheasant's egg; you must not gather a bluebell. In fact you must not do anything, by word or look or deed, even in innocence, to upset the course of the drama in which he is a star performer.

Among the many components of the English countryside Bates considers the wood to be the most beautiful, but he does not disconnect it from the landscape. He makes frequent reference to adjoining features and terrain: cornfields, rivers and hedgerows, even a much larger woodland sprawled over the hills above. These elements give context and contrast and add colour to the little wood, making them part of its story. A particularly illuminating passage, for example, details the effect created by a bordering stream:

> This fusion of wood and water is an entrancing thing. Without the wood the stream would be nothing . . . But water and wood, together, shading and watering and bounding each other, each give to the other something which the other does not possess, the wood giving to the stream something solid and shadowy and

immemorial, the stream giving to the wood all the incomparable movement and twinkling transience of moving water.

Bates wrote that the best woods are small, ideally only a few acres, 'not much more than copses'. Forests, on the other hand, are something quite different; they go on and on, he concludes, 'like the vast bulk of an unread book'.

As I see it, prose can never overrate the wood: the small intimate English wood with its variation of trees, its many flowers and bird voices, its feeling of being only a part but never the whole of a countryside. It never dominates, never assumes the dark dictatorship of forests. You can walk in it and through it and round it without a sense of oppression, a sense of its being too great for you. At the same time its life is quick and, at its best, stimulating and entrancing. It is never dead, not even dormant.

This to me is a wonderful comparison, and a metaphor for his own literary approach – not least his inclination towards the drama of the short story. The little English wood is a novella, not an epic, but it concentrates within its small acreage stories of epic and noble proportions.

MATT COLLINS is Head Gardener at the Garden Museum in London and a writer on landscape and gardens. His new book, *Forest: Walking among Trees*, traces an intercontinental pathway between trees and their wilder wooded contexts.

Mood Music

REBECCA WILLIS

Until I read the bit in Rebecca West's *This Real Night* where one of
the main characters dies, I'd never cried properly on a plane. I'll
admit to a bit of panicky sobbing during a bout of bad turbulence,
but never before had I abandoned myself to full-on, uncontrollable
weeping at 33,000 feet.

I won't tell you which of the characters dies, because that would
be a cruel spoiler, and I am hoping to persuade you to spend time
with this strange, wonderful trilogy and the eccentric Aubrey family
who live in its pages. But I'm getting ahead of myself, because *This
Real Night* is the second book in the series and – like the unfinished
third, *Cousin Rosamund* – was published posthumously (1984 and
1985 respectively). I often feel a twinge of guilt when I read a book
that the author had not wanted published in his or her lifetime: it
seems somehow disrespectful. West, who died at the age of 90 in
1983, had had at least two decades to change her mind about these
two if she'd wanted to. But in this case I didn't even hesitate. As soon
as I'd finished the first book, *The Fountain Overflows* (1957), I was
sucked into the second like air into a vacuum.

The three books together were to be known, somewhat hubristic-
ally, as 'The Saga of the Century'; in fact they only cover the first half
of the twentieth century, not least because the second half hadn't yet

Rebecca West's *The Fountain Overflows* (1957) is available as a Virago Modern
Classic · Pb · 448pp · £10.99 · ISBN 9781844086993; *This Real Night* (1984)
and *Cousin Rosamund* (1985) are out of print but we can obtain second-hand
copies.

happened. They are West's fictionalized autobiography, narrated in the first person by Rose, who is a young girl when *The Fountain Overflows* begins. We do not immediately learn her exact age and only eventually do we work out that her sister Mary is her twin – West doesn't bother much with external details, she just plunges the reader straight into the peculiar life of the family.

This is the opening sentence: 'There was such a long pause that I wondered whether my Mamma and my Papa were ever going to speak to one another again.' Papa is the black sheep of an Irish land-owning family, a brilliant but improvident journalist who gambles and speculates with any money that comes his way. He is a passionate espouser of public causes but completely ignores his responsibilities to his family. (The children adore him, not least because he builds entrancing wooden models for their Christmas presents, but he is also capable of selling his wife's prized furniture without her permission.) Mamma is a former concert pianist, sensitive but strong, who nurtures her children's musical abilities while just managing to maintain the household in a sort of shabby gentility on very slender means. Her character is the keystone of the book.

So far, so close to West's own parents: her father left the family when she was 8 and died impoverished when she was 14; in the book the father stays until the children are in their late teens. West, like Rose, had two sisters, but Rose is also given a younger brother called Richard Quin, a figure of unusual charm and goodness who is a counterpoint to the feckless father. It is impossible not to fall for Richard Quin, but at the same time one cannot help feeling that he is there to act as a cypher for the whole generation of innocent young men whose lives were about to be ruined by the First World War. And possibly, also, to rewrite West's disastrous relationship with her own son, Anthony, from her ten-year affair with the married H. G. Wells.

The gap between Rose's child's-eye observations of her parents' marriage and our own adult understanding of the situation is what gives the book much of its poignancy. But it is never cloying – as child narrators can so easily be – and is often extremely funny. One of its themes is the relationship between childhood and adulthood. Mamma, for instance, 'understood children, and knew that they were adults handicapped by a humiliating disguise and had their adult qualities within them'. I wish I'd read that sentence when I was 12. Rose recognizes in cousin Rosamund, who is a similar age, 'that she was in the same case as myself, as every child I liked, she found childhood an embarrassing state. We did not like wearing ridiculous clothes, and being ordered about by people whom we often recognized as stupid and horrid.'

It makes sense to look at the book in terms of its themes because – although there are events, some of them dramatic – plot is not what drives it forward. It is an atmosphere which you inhale and which intoxicates and casts its hypnotic spell over you. To me it recreates how growing up and being part of a family actually feels. There is a big revelation towards the end – both parents have kept a secret from each other – but to call it a plot twist would be going too far. Like learning something new about your parents in real life, it changes your view of the past, but doesn't change the past itself.

The Fountain Overflows explores the relationship between life and art, between real and false art, and what it means to be an artist. The art here is music, but we intuit that it stands also for writing, for art of all kinds. Mamma gave up her promising career as a concert pianist and although she is worn out by her husband's neglect, she is sustained by music: the family views those who live without art as the real paupers of this world. Rose and Mary have inherited her skill and plan to be concert pianists themselves – as the book ends they are heading off with scholarships to different schools of music in London.

Cordelia, the eldest daughter, plays the violin and – encouraged by her teacher, Miss Beevor – begins to perform for money. She feels the burden of the family's poverty and sees a way of helping the family and escaping from her circumstances. But Mamma and the twins know that her abilities are limited. Eventually a maestro confronts Cordelia with the truth and she never plays again, instead settling for a conventional, bourgeois marriage which the rest of the family regard with horror. The deluded Miss Beevor is at first a figure of mockery, but over time compassionate Mamma enfolds her, as she enfolds other characters and indeed the reader, into the warmth and spiritual generosity of the family.

Supernatural happenings recur and are treated as matter-of-factly as having breakfast. When Rose and her mother go to visit cousin Constance and her daughter Rosamund, they are greeted by a fireside poker punching a hole in the window. The house is under siege from a poltergeist: saucepans and crockery fly about, a deafening tattoo is beaten out on the flour bin, bits of coal rain down, sash windows open and close. Its presence in this house, where Constance's mean and controlling husband also lives, has meant that they spend all their time clearing up and mending things, and cannot make friends. But it all stops suddenly because 'to drive out the evil presence it had been needed simply that we four should be in a room together, nothing more'. The power of love, perhaps? Certainly Constance and Rosamund are rescued, and they come to stay with the family in the fading old villa in south London, which Papa's Uncle Ralph has mercifully allowed them to rent.

The power of sisterhood is strong in this book; men almost always get a poor showing. Their lot improves somewhat in *This Real Night*, mostly because Papa does not appear in the second book and instead we get to know his generous and cultured patron, Mr Morpurgo. By now the family finances have become easier. Curious characters and period detail spring from the page, there are rural idylls as well as city life, and the twins continue with their music, but the approach of the First World War is inexorable and devastating. It feels like a completed book, whereas the third, *Cousin Rosamund*, is formless and evidently unfinished. Rosamund, gentle and infinitely patient and good, makes such an inexplicable marriage that I speculated as to whether West simply felt defeated by her own creation. Why had she written it – to show, perhaps, that people we love can drift away from us into other worlds even while still on this earth? We will never know, and the book is, inevitably, unsatisfying. Even so, it does give us powerful passages on finding love and living life after great loss.

The epigraph to the first book reveals the origin of the novel's title, from William Blake's 'Proverbs of Hell': 'the cistern contains, the fountain overflows'. The only fountain repeatedly mentioned appears on a brooch worn by the pathetic Miss Beevor, 'a mosaic representing two doves drinking from a fountain', at which Mamma stares with 'a positive grimace of disapproval'. This leitmotif may represent false or pretentious art, but it also calls to mind the twins imbibing their mother's music lessons. After wrestling with it for a bit, I take the title to mean that the subject is the interplay of freedom and restriction in many areas of life, but

Rebecca West by Wyndham Lewis, pencil, 1932

above all that it is a hymn to the creative impulse. The book is engrossing whatever the title means.

Rebecca West was born Cicely Isabel Fairfield, but it was not until I encountered the rebellious heroine of Ibsen's *Rosmersholm* – the mistress of a married man – that I realized she had taken a pseudonym. *The Fountain Overflows* is dedicated to her sister, Letitia Fairfield, who was a doctor, a lawyer and the first female Chief Medical Officer for London. She was also the model for Cordelia and, not entirely surprisingly, she hated the book.

In 1947, *Time* magazine described West as 'indisputably the world's number one woman writer'. You can't help wondering how that qualifier sounded to the former suffragette, but it reminds us what a towering figure she was in her time. A pioneering feminist and a Fabian socialist, she was best known for her factual writing, her literary criticism and her journalism (which included reporting from the Nuremberg trials), as well as for her complicated and ultimately un-fulfilling private life. H. G. Wells wrote of West: 'I had never met any-thing like her before, and I doubt if there was anything like her before.'

That is how I feel about *The Fountain Overflows*: it is *sui generis*. I can't think of another book that has woven around me such a curious and particular web of enchantment. It is one of those that, when you are reading it, lives inside your head as much as the actual world you are forced to inhabit. I suspect that it resonates most with those who come from big or close or complicated families, or who are at least interested in what that might feel like. West understands that those we are closest to can still be alien or utterly mysterious. She under-stands the silken ties and dark magic that bind a family.

REBECCA WILLIS occasionally gets called 'Rebecca West' which, although always a slip of the tongue, she considers the greatest possible compliment.

The portrait of Rebecca West is reproduced by kind permisssion of the Wynd-ham Lewis Memorial Trust (NPG © Wyndham Lewis and the Estate of the late Mrs G. A. Lewis).

An Olympian Effort

PETER RADFORD

When I was a young man I was an international runner who held world sprint records and won medals in the European Championships, the Commonwealth Games and the Olympic Games. You would be right in thinking that training, allied with natural ability, had something to do with this, but it was a book, bought when I was 13, that made it all possible. That book changed my life.

It all began in 1952, when I was 12 and won the Under-13 100 yards race at my school sports day. That victory gave me an identity – I was a sprinter. The year 1952 was an Olympic one and the newspapers were full of stories about the athletes who would go to Helsinki to represent Britain, including sprinters, most notably E. McDonald Bailey, a native of Trinidad, who was the current AAA 100 yards champion. *Picture Post* carried a double-page spread of him leaving the starting blocks. I cut it out and pasted it on to thick white paper, making my own poster of him. Other pictures (all of McDonald Bailey) followed and soon I had a gallery on my bedroom wall. On 21 July, I remember listening to his Olympic 100 metres Final on the BBC Home Service. He finished third and so won the Bronze medal and came back to Britain with his head held high; only Foxhunter, a horse, had won a Gold for Britain at the Games.

The next summer, now aged 13, I didn't add any new sprint successes to my previous year's tally; my sprinting career was on hold. I still hung on to my (silently) self-declared identity as a sprinter,

E. McDonald Bailey, *If It's Speed You're After* (1953), is out of print but we can obtain second-hand copies.

though no one else would have recognized it; my home town had no running track, and so no athletics club or coach. My school was three bus rides away, and there was no running track there either. It took about an hour and a quarter for me to get to school each day. I left the house at about 7.45 but seldom managed to scramble downstairs much before 7.30, gobbled some breakfast and was gone.

One morning in June I rushed downstairs and said to my mother, 'I had a dream last night.'

'Oh?' came the reply.

'Yes, I dreamt that Choir Boy will win the National Hunt Cup,' I said, and with that I left.

At the end of the week, when I normally got my half-crown pocket money before going to school, my mother handed me £1 7s 6d, eleven times what I expected. 'Choir Boy', she said, 'won at 10 to 1.'

'10 to 1?' I asked, bemused.

'Yes, you get ten times your bet, and you get your original stake back,' . . . and with that, it was again time to go and catch the first of my buses.

My mother had put my pocket money on a horse? That would probably be a surprising, perhaps even shocking, event in most families, but in mine it was extraordinary. We were Quakers. We didn't gamble, we didn't go to the races, we didn't even *talk* about racing or racehorses. And, incidentally, we didn't drink or swear. I was stunned. How had she done it? There were no betting shops on the high street then, only grey-looking men on street corners, in cloth caps, with a cigarette hanging from their lower lip; surely my mother hadn't handed my half-crown to one of them? Most unsettling of all, though, was how had I known which horse was going to win? I still don't know the answer and, sad to report, it never happened again.

However, I now had money in my hand. With it I went to W. H. Smith's and bought a book that I knew was sitting on its shelves – *If It's Speed You're After* by E. McDonald Bailey. Published that year, it was pocket-sized, with photographs and comical line drawings, and a foreword by Philip Noel-Baker, an Olympic medallist, a prominent politician and a Quaker, and it cost 6 shillings. I took it home and devoured every word of it.

On line three of the first page McDonald Bailey gets down to basics:

> I hope I may encourage you to take up the hard work that goes to make a top-class athlete, and if you don't reach Olympic standard you may well become the fastest runner in your club, or in your town, or in your county.
>
> I said something about hard work. Don't let that scare you, but I cannot emphasise too soon or too strongly that only by hard work can you hope to reach, or even to approach, the top. Rigid self-discipline, a willingness to learn, a determination not to be discouraged by early setbacks – these are the prerequisites of success as a sprinter, or of anything else, come to think of it.

This was all very well, but with no coach, no club and no track, how was I to follow his advice? At that stage in my life I had not even *seen* a running track, except in pictures.

It was now the middle of June. A month later school finished for the summer holidays. On the last day, and after the last lesson, we lined up alongside our desks waiting to be dismissed. My classroom was on the first floor of a Victorian building known as The Towers. Large sash windows at the back opened on to a fire escape. As the others surged forward, eager to go, I quietly made my way to the back of the room and undid the lock on one of the sash windows. I then followed the rest of the boys out and caught the first of my buses home.

After a few days hanging around the house, I packed my shorts, vest and pumps into a bag, slipped *If It's Speed You're After* into my pocket, and set off for school. Once through the gates, I quickly made my way to the back of The Towers, climbed the fire escape and, finding the window unlocked as I had left it, climbed in. The main school building was some distance away and screened by shrubs, so no one saw my arrival or my climb back down the fire escape, now changed into shorts and vest and clutching my book. No one saw me go down to the playing fields and place my book on the grass, open it at the chosen page and start to train.

I never told anyone where I went or what I did that summer, not until decades later. But the following year I won all my races, and within five years I had broken every British sprint record. I had acquired a coach and a club, and a running track had been built near my school. And at the age of 20 I came home from the Rome Olympics with a Bronze medal for the 100 metres, just as McDonald Bailey had done.

It would be easy to dismiss *If It's Speed You're After* as a mere 'how to' book, but books are often not about what they tell you to do, but about what they make you think. McDonald Bailey wrote about training, diet and injuries, but also about attitudes of mind, and the relationship between the crowd and the performer. He also asked awkward questions such as 'What is sportsmanship?' He even attempted to face head-on the issue of black sprinters' success. 'Have you ever wondered', he wrote, 'why coloured athletes excel . . . particularly in sprinting?' In trying to answer that question he looked at racial differences in patella tendon reflexes, the length of tendons in the heel, heredity, history and sunshine. 'Perhaps even white athletes', he concluded, 'with sunshine in their bones can match the speed of the negro sprinter.' I read with fascination that he wanted to see an end to such typical remarks of the time as 'Oh, he's bound to win – he's a darkie,' partly because it was not always true, and partly because it was bad psychologically for white sprinters. There was certainly a lot to think about here for a boy of 13, and it has kept me thinking ever since.

If It's Speed You're After still sits on my bookshelves sixty-five years after its first appearance there. Small, slim and modest, it has joined that magical circle of books that have been there so long they seem now to radiate their messages without even having to be opened. *Work hard, be willing to learn, and don't be put off by apparently over-whelming odds,* it says. But it also carries reminders of a schoolboy's dream, and of a young Queen. The horse that won me the money to buy the book was owned by Her Majesty and won for her, and for me, and against the odds, only a few days after her coronation. This is almost the first time I have told this story – almost but not quite. I have told the Queen.

This article was a runner-up in our 2018 writers' competition. PETER RADFORD was Titular Professor at the University of Glasgow and Professor of Sport Sciences at Brunel University, before he retired. He now lives in the Cotswolds.

Scoops of the Century

ANTHONY WELLS

'Deutschland über Alles' can hardly be a frequent selection on *Desert Island Discs*. But in 1999, it was the second pick of foreign correspondent extraordinary Clare Hollingworth, then aged 88, for whom it triggered memories of her two 'scoops of the century' sixty years before. The first was in late August 1939, when she drove across the Polish-German border in a borrowed official car and spotted scores of German tanks lined up facing Poland. The second followed a few days later when, woken by anti-aircraft fire, she rang her paper's senior correspondent in Warsaw with the news that the war had started. When he told her he didn't believe her, she held the telephone out of the window to catch the sound of exploding German bombs. Not bad for a cub reporter on her first foreign assignment.

Her next assignment was to be rather longer in duration and only marginally less dangerous: a commission to write a book about Romania. The result was *There's a German Just Behind Me*, the catchily (and aptly) titled book that covered her Balkan travels between the fall of France in June 1940 and the invasion of Russia a year later when, as she writes in the preface, 'the Balkan states were the principal object of Germany's designs'. As such, the region was of interest to other powers: Britain was anxious to keep the Axis's hands off Romanian oil and protect British territories in the Eastern Mediterranean; Russia was concerned for her fellow Slavs in Bulgaria and Yugoslavia; and Italy, having occupied Albania, now had her eye

---

Clare Hollingworth, *There's a German Just Behind Me* (1943), is out of print. Second-hand copies are scarce.

on Greece. The Balkans were obviously the place for a keen young reporter like Hollingworth to be, with her knowledge of the region (acquired by poring over maps of the Balkans as a child) and her single-minded dedication to 'the story'.

Journalism has been called the first rough draft of history and while Hollingworth's book certainly reads like journalism – it was written at speed, by someone also working as a reporter – it will just as certainly remain a valuable source for future historians. For readers who are not professional historians, it is fair to say that a little previous knowledge of pre-war Balkan history is useful. It is handy if such names as Antonescu, Horia Silva, Metaxas and Venizelos ring some kind of bell. Even handier is a map of south-eastern Europe, or two – a present-day one and, if you can find it, a pre-war edition. Here's why. In a chance encounter on a cross-Channel ferry in 1936, Clare is told by a fellow traveller: 'Watch Cernauti! The first great clash of the Second World War will occur there.' Cernauti? There's no Cernauti on my map that I can see. A quick Internet search is needed to reveal that Cernauti in Romania is now Chernivsti in Ukraine (and before being Cernauti in Romania was Czernowitz in Austro-Hungary).

Fortunately, our author is an excellent guide, if not so much to the geography (since she takes for granted that you are familiar with it) then to the politics, the places and the people. She is brisk, forthright, daring and with not a drop of sentimentality in her veins, all of which make her an exhilarating and incisive guide to the often squalid and volatile Balkan scene in these months before the Wehrmacht arrived. To convey her style, here's an extract from one of her chapters on Romania, the country which, with Greece, most fascinated her. Arriving in Bucharest in June 1940, she finds the city enjoying 'the same gay life' as when she was there at the beginning of the war. Beneath all the gaiety, though, it is quite obvious that things had been going wrong.

The British Minister, Sir Reginald Hoare, had lost a great deal of his power. Before the war began he had been an intimate friend of Armand Calinescu, prime minister until his assassination just after the downfall of Poland . . . A few days after I had left Poland, on my way out to lunch, I was held up by a crowd; they were explaining how a farmer's cart had blocked the route of the Prime Minister's car on his way home from lunch, and whilst the luxury car was slowing down his body and that of his private detective had been riddled with bullets by the Iron Guard. Calinescu was immediately made a public hero; his body was laid out in state surrounded by candles, dressed in purple velvet. The members of the Iron Guard who shot him were taken out in a lorry to the spot where the incident happened, and were there shot one by one, with half an hour's interval between each shooting. Their dead bodies were allowed to lie in the dust for forty-eight hours; newsvendors, orange sellers, gipsy fortune-tellers, and particularly sellers of hot food did a great trade meanwhile.

This passage has all the hallmarks of Hollingworth's reportage: her knowledge, often personal, of the individuals; her knack of being near the centre of the action; her detail; and her matter-of-fact observation of the nastier sides of human nature. She is also keen to record the 'human interest' side. After the loss of Calinescu, Sir Reginald Hoare established close contact with Gafencu, the Romanian foreign secretary. 'Gafencu', Hollingworth writes with characteristic candour, 'is physically one of the most attractive men I have ever had the good fortune to see. He married when young a Frenchwoman, who it is said was brought to Bucharest as the mistress of an elderly rich industrialist who tired of her. She then became a cabaret dancer, and, rumour has it, used to be carried naked on a pseudo-golden plate into one of the night-clubs of Bucharest.' But Hollingworth's last word is kept for the politician. Gafencu, she writes, 'is a man of convictions, but not of convictions sufficient to carry him through the

German political attack on Romania'. It will be a failure repeated across the region, as leader after Balkan leader fails to put up any resistance to the German advance – at first clandestine, then open – and is mirrored, in Hollingworth's trenchantly expressed view, by the failure of the majority of British officials to defend their country's interests there.

The directness of Hollingworth's opinions on public matters is echoed in her brisk approach to her own personal comfort and safety, whether in grubby hotel rooms or roughing it on the Albanian front.

 In the course of her book, we learn variously that our reporter always carries a revolver (and at times three), can sleep anywhere, including on a stone floor, is not bothered by fewer than twenty bed bugs at a time, never catches a cold and has a very hard head when it comes to drink (to be tested later in Beirut in the company of Kim Philby, whose departure to the USSR was another scoop of hers). Aspiring young foreign correspondents take note!

Her tone of authority extends to more mundane matters, too. Lavatories, for instance (these in Chisinau in Bessarabia) –

The water-closets at the Hotel Londra, the best in the place, are repellent even by Balkan standards

– brothels (this in a Greek town recently abandoned by Italian troops) –

I walked through the passages and looked into many of the deserted rooms. They were cleaner than I expected, devoid of the pink lighting effects so noticeable in the brothels in Romania.

– and, last but not least, fascist parades, these being from Romania in September 1940:

They reminded me very much of the Fascist processions I used unwillingly to watch on Sunday afternoons while waiting for a bus in King's Road, Chelsea. In Bucharest as in Chelsea, the longer the procession, the pimplier the youths.

Le style c'est l'homme, or in this case *la femme* – the whole robust, no-nonsense, clear-sighted foreign correspondent is right there.

Clare Hollingworth lived to the high old age of 105, spending much of her last years in the Foreign Correspondents' Club in her adopted home of Hong Kong. Even at the age of 92 she was said to be prepared to head out to whatever hot-spot her editor might want to send her to. After reading *There's a German Just Behind Me*, you'll rather wish her editor had given her the call.

ANTHONY WELLS spent five years covering the Balkans for BBC Monitoring in the 1990s. Unlike Clare Hollingworth's, his was a safe, desk-bound job where the only hardship was the coffee in the BBC canteen.

Ire and Irritability

PAULINE MELVILLE

I am having another stab at Jane Austen.

Friends beg me to keep trying, anxious for me not to miss what they tell me is an unrivalled view of a luminous literary landscape. I have made efforts on and off over the years and never found her to my taste. Somewhere along the line at school I passed through *Northanger Abbey* without retaining much impression of it. But now I have made a pledge with a friend who works at the Royal Society of Literature. I must endeavour to read some Austen and my friend will attempt to read *Wuthering Heights*, a book she has heretofore avoided. She suggested I start with *Sense and Sensibility*, so I did.

Well, there are certainly notable descriptions of handsome houses, mansions set in parkland and snug but sensible cottages. By chapter five of *Sense and Sensibility* I am wondering whether or not Austen should have been an estate agent. The division of an estate, the properties, the provisions of a will, its legal intricacies, the inheritance – all of which Austen understood well – the landed gentry, all these are hitting a nerve. Images of precise but insipid watercolours float across my mind alongside scenes costumed by Laura Ashley.

Daniel Macklin

Jane Austen, *Sense and Sensibility* (1811)
Vintage · Pb · 464pp · £7.99 · ISBN 9780099589341

The truth is I am already trying to suppress a mounting fury, the source of which I cannot fathom. However, I do appreciate the brevity of the chapters. I must remember that as a useful technique for encouraging a reader to continue.

Why the fury? I start to examine my extreme and visceral reaction to various kinds of literature and am surprised to realize how far back it goes. I could not have been more than 5 when I took an intense dislike to the nursery rhyme 'A frog he would a-wooing go'. We sang it regularly at school. I try to remember now why I disliked it so much. After all, I liked the song about the old woman who swallowed a fly. I enjoyed the satisfying menace of the Teddy Bear's Picnic. But I hated the amorous frog. I took a violent antipathy to the character, the song and its silly chorus. Frankly, I found it childish.

At the other extreme, I was passionately engaged by a series of books about a small koala bear called Wonk which I was just able to read for myself. I can still see the illustrations – Wonk leaning over the side of a ship with his scarf fluttering; Wonk discovering a nice place to sleep on board, a cabin with a large bed and a salmon-coloured silk bedspread. I am not sure if he had run away to sea and whether that was the origin of my own attempts to escape. But to this end I kept a small and scuffed brown suitcase under the bed. It contained my red woollen polo-necked sweater and nothing else. It was my running-away kit. I took off more than once with my little suitcase, informing any neighbour I passed that I was running away. No one seemed bothered. I can't remember where I went or how long I was away. But I do remember that when I returned, no one noticed that I'd gone.

Our household did not contain books. One day my Auntie Ella heard that for the first time there were going to be Penguins in Selfridges. Assuming it was some sort of new zoo department, she rounded us children up and took us to Oxford Street: 'There you are,' she said, refusing to acknowledge her mistake and addressing a group of disgruntled and disappointed children: 'There are the penguins,' and we were obliged to examine the tiny image of a penguin printed on the spine of each orange and white book. Fortunately for me, there was a wonderful Carnegie library not far from us and I spent much of my time there.

Looking back on my own history in relation to books it is likely that I shared with many others a flaring of rage when Jo March, the aspiring writer in *Little Women*, hooked up with dull, bearded Professor Bhaer. I liked tomboyish Jo although I did not think then that writing could be a satisfying occupation. I had my eye on becoming a trapeze artist. And the professor with the unpronounceable name was the pits.

But this does bring up the question: when does a reader become aware that there is a writer? Child readers enter the magical world of a book without realizing that someone has written it. I remember an early experience of my own awareness of the writer. In the story I was reading I came across the word 'pasty' – unsurprising seeing that the story was set in Cornwall and the object in question was a Cornish pasty. But I could not believe that someone had been unable to spell 'pastry'. It was shocking to find such a mistake. Some enchantment was broken and I was shaken out of the world of the story to realize that there were other people behind the book, people who operated printing machines, a writer who couldn't spell pastry. It was somewhat akin to the discovery that the wizardry in *The Wizard of Oz* was only the mechanical trickery of an ordinary man.

I am now at chapter fifteen of *Sense and Sensibility* and am becoming more engaged by Austen's shrewd observation of character and astute, understated wit. Both Willoughby and Colonel Brandon have made mysterious departures. I sense careful plotting as in a chess game, the pieces gliding from one point to another, some characters making unexpected moves forward or sideways guided by a firm but unseen hand and sometimes, with a swoop, disappearing from the board altogether. I notice the chapters are getting longer.

There is a parlour game: Are you for Austen or Brontë? Are you for Tolstoy or Dostoevsky? It comes down to whether you are, by temperament, Apollonian or Dionysiac, whether you prefer the beauty of order to the explosion of order. On reading Austen's *Pride and Prejudice*, Charlotte Brontë found only 'a commonplace face; a carefully fenced, highly cultivated garden, with neat borders and delicate flowers'. D. H. Lawrence called Jane Austen 'English in the bad, mean, snobbish sense of the word'. A puzzled Joseph Conrad asked H. G. Wells, 'What is there in her? What is it all about?' Vladimir Nabokov told a critic: 'I dislike Jane . . . could never see anything in *Pride and Prejudice.*'

Now I am at chapter twenty-one. Two more smart ladies have arrived to talk of eligible acquaintances and marriageable beaux. Nobody seems to go to work. Their life is a ceaseless social round, punctuated by walks or drives in the countryside. There is not even a far-distant echo of the French Revolution or the Napoleonic wars, and not a hint of the slave trade which probably funded some of the landowners who grace these pages.

Perhaps it is unfair to criticize an author for the lack of something he or she never intended. Austen did not aim to write anything profound. She was not a tragedian. Having said that, I've just reached chapter thirty-one and illegitimacy, consumption and death have put in an unexpected appearance. But they are soon passed over in favour of the pains of unrequited love, being jilted, and the worry of who might be two-timing whom. All the same, my fury is subsiding. Austen's deft touch with social manners is unsurpassed. To be observant and entertaining was enough for her. I am enjoying the book and am beginning to appreciate the nice distinctions between being betrayed, dumped, slighted, misled or simply mistaken.

Now we are at chapter thirty-four and despite the despair, heartbreak and deception I have a horrible feeling that all is going to work out well.

By chapter thirty-seven, a long chapter much concerned with the value of estates and settlements and prospects and the financial requirements of any liaison, I am beginning to wonder if I have mistaken Austen for a High Tory when she is, in fact, a precocious Marxist, agreeing with the construct that the economic base determines the ideological superstructure. After all, throughout the novel there are delicate, well-defined attacks on the bourgeoisie, although the satirical pin-pricks would not cause much damage to any Gulliverian hide.

Chapter forty-three. Marianne is desperately ill. Could a death be in the offing? No such luck.

I see why I myself might have been the object of Austen's derision. Undoubtedly, she had a healthy reaction to the burlesque and melodrama popular in her time: maybe I have some leanings towards the Gothic romances that she mocked.

Now I have finished the book and am more than half won over, although somewhere, at the back of my mind, is the feeling of still wanting to upturn the chessboard. However, I would not go as far as Mark Twain who, on reading *Pride and Prejudice*, said of Austen that it made him 'want to dig her up and beat her over the skull with her own shin-bone'.

My friend has just told me that it wasn't *Sense and Sensibility* at all that she recommended. It was *Persuasion*. I find I'm ready to discard both my pride and my prejudices and give it a try.

Having failed to pursue a career as a trapeze artist and having turned down the opportunity to tour with Bertram Mills Circus in favour of joining the National Theatre, PAULINE MELVILLE now confines herself to flights of fiction, short stories and novels, some award-winning and some not.

Bibliography

Coming attractions

D. J. TAYLOR finds romance on an Ayrshire farm · JACQUELINE WILSON puts on her ballet shoes · PATRICK WELLAND joins the British Council · MIRANDA SEYMOUR relishes the twilight hour · CHRISTOPHER RUSH goes back to 1984 · AMANDA THEUNISSEN discovers there's *No Bed for Bacon* · TIM MACKINTOSH-SMITH learns to read under the piano · SUE GEE follows Roald Dahl to school · ALAN BRADLEY meets some remarkable manuscripts

BY APPOINTMENT TO
HER MAJESTY THE QUEEN
PURVEYORS OF RARE BOOKS
& MANUSCRIPTS
MAGGS BROS. LTD LONDON

MAGGS BROS. LTD.
RARE BOOKS & MANUSCRIPTS

EST. 1853

MAGGS BLOOMSBURY
48 BEDFORD SQUARE
WCIB 3DR

MAGGS MAYFAIR
46 CURZON STREET
WIJ 7UH

T: +44(0) 207 493 7160 · WWW.MAGGS.COM
E: ENQUIRIES@MAGGS.COM